Taste of Home
30-MINUTE
MEALS

TASTE OF HOME BOOKS • RDA ENTHUSIAST BRANDS, LLC • MILWAUKEE, WI

© 2020 RDA Enthusiast Brands, LLC.
1610 N. 2nd St., Suite 102,
Milwaukee WI 53212-3906

Visit us at **tasteofhome.com** for other
Taste of Home books and products.

International Standard Book Number:
978-1-61765-912-6
Library of Congress Control Number:
2019950031
Component Number: 118600023H

Executive Editor: Mark Hagen
Senior Art Director: Raeann Thompson
Editor: Amy Glander
Designers: Arielle Jardine, Jazmin Delgado
Copy Editor: Amy Rabideau Silvers

Cover Photography:
Taste of Home Photo Studio

Pictured on front cover:
Bavarian Apple-Sausage Hash, p. 149
Pictured on title page:
Pressure-Cooker Carolina-Style
Vinegar BBQ Chicken, p. 87
Pictured on back cover:
One-Pot Spinach Beef Soup, p. 68
Chicken with Peach-Cucumber Salsa, p. 169
Grilled Banana Brownie Sundaes, p. 236
Pictured on spine:
Calzone Pinwheels, p. 44

Printed in USA
1 3 5 7 9 10 8 6 4 2

243

MORE WAYS TO CONNECT WITH US:

CONTENTS

AT-A-GLANCE ICONS:

A five-ingredient icon indicates recipes that call for 5 or fewer ingredients (not including water, salt, pepper, oils or optional items). A freezer icon indicates recipes that can be made ahead and frozen.

DINNER JUST GOT EASIER!

For those days when life is a whirlwind, rely on these timesaving recipes for quick home-style dinners. Your family will be thrilled with the delicious results, and you'll be out of the kitchen in 30 minutes—or less!

83

Dig in! Here you'll find 115 flavorful recipes that come together when a tasty meal is top priority but time isn't on your side. Not only are these quick-to-fix favorites table-ready in a pinch, but they call for everyday ingredients, satisfy the whole gang and come from the kitchens of today's family cooks. These busy chefs know what it's like to make dinner in short order and have generously shared their most-requested dishes here.

Turn the page for a mouthwatering variety of entrees. From beef and chicken to pork and fish, you'll always find the ideal recipe. Looking for a casual dish? Give Asparagus Ham Dinner a try. Need to impress guests but don't want to fuss? Whip up Blue Cheese-Crusted Sirloin Steaks. There's also sides, breads, breakfast entrees, desserts and more to make it a snap to build exciting menus and satisfy hunger one easy meal at a time.

178

103

235

STOCKING UP & STORAGE GUIDELINES

Stocking the pantry, refrigerator and freezer with the ingredients and foods you use most often can simplify menu planning and preparation.

Trim grocery bills and beat the clock by stocking up on your go-to ingredients. Keep frequently used fresh produce in the refrigerator and shelf-stable packaged and canned goods in the pantry. Always keep a variety of meat, poultry and seafood in the freezer.

PANTRY STORAGE

- Periodically check the sell-by or use-by dates on packaged goods and discard what's expired.
- Store opened boxes and bags tightly closed in a cool, dry place.

REFRIGERATED FOOD

The use-by date on refrigerated items is for unopened items.

- Keep the refrigerator temperature between 34° and 40°.
- Store food in covered containers, sustainable food storage bags or wrap it in aluminum foil.

FROZEN FOOD

To maintain the best quality in frozen foods, set the freezer to 0°. Don't fill it more than two-thirds full.

- Cooked food should be cooled completely before being placed in the freezer. Placing warm food in the freezer can result in bacteria growth.
- Package foods in freezer containers or materials that help prevent mixed odors and moisture loss, such as foil, freezer bags or wrap, or airtight freezer containers.
- Remove as much air as possible from the package, seal it, then label and date. Spread out packages when freezing and stack them only after they are frozen.
- Defrost frozen foods in the refrigerator, in a microwave or in cold water. Most items will need a day or two in the refrigerator; bulky, heavy items may take longer. If defrosting in the microwave, follow the manufacturer's directions. For cold-water thawing, place food in a watertight plastic bag and submerge it in cold water until defrosted, changing the water every 30 minutes.

10 Things You Should Always Have in Your Kitchen

You can get several dinner recipes started with these common kitchen staples.

- Diced Tomatoes
- Mixed Veggies
- Broth
- Rice
- Potatoes
- Meatballs
- Pasta Sauce
- Beans
- Corn
- Pasta

SHEEPHERDER'S
BREAKFAST, 32

CHAPTER 1

BREAKFAST FAVORITES

Busy mornings got you hustling? Don't skip breakfast. Stave off hunger until the noon bell rings with these lightning-fast dishes.

BAKED BLUEBERRY GINGER PANCAKE

My kids love pancakes, so I came up with this ginger-kissed baked version
that saves a lot of time on hectic mornings. They gobble this right up!

—*Erin Wright, Wallace, KS*

TAKES: 30 min. • **MAKES:** 9 servings

2 large eggs,
   room temperature
1½ cups 2% milk
¼ cup butter, melted
2 cups all-purpose flour
2 Tbsp. sugar
3 tsp. baking powder
1½ tsp. ground ginger
½ tsp. salt
2 cups fresh or frozen
   unsweetened blueberries
   Maple syrup

1. Preheat oven to 350°. Combine eggs, milk and butter. Whisk the next 5 ingredients; add to egg mixture. Spoon batter into a 9-in. square baking pan coated with cooking spray. Sprinkle blueberries over top.

2. Bake until a toothpick inserted in the center comes out clean, 20-25 minutes. Cut into squares; serve with warm maple syrup.

1 PIECE: 213 cal., 7g fat (4g sat. fat), 58mg chol., 368mg sod., 31g carb. (8g sugars, 2g fiber), 6g pro. *Diabetic exchanges:* 2 starch, 1½ fat.

TEST KITCHEN TIP

If little ones aren't fans of ginger, feel free to scale it back or replace it with something else, such as ground cinnamon or grated lemon zest.

SUNNY-SIDE-UP PIZZA

If I want my family to eat a good breakfast, I make something I know will pull them out of bed. This recipe does the trick. I just call out "Pizza's ready!" and everyone comes to the table.

—*Rose Koren, Brookfield, IL*

TAKES: 30 min. • **MAKES:** 6 servings

1 prebaked 12-in. thin pizza crust

6 large eggs

1½ cups shredded part-skim mozzarella cheese

8 bacon strips, cooked and crumbled

½ cup chopped sweet red pepper

½ cup chopped green pepper

1 small onion, chopped

Preheat oven to 450°. Place crust on a greased pizza pan. Using a 2½-in. biscuit cutter, cut out 6 circles from crust. (Remove circles and save for another use.) Break an egg into each hole. Sprinkle with cheese, bacon, peppers and onion. Bake until eggs are completely set, 8-10 minutes.

1 SLICE: 355 cal., 18g fat (7g sat. fat), 242mg chol., 578mg sod., 27g carb. (3g sugars, 2g fiber), 20g pro.

READER RAVE

"This is such a fun breakfast! We used one whole red pepper, since that is what we had."

—THERESA, TASTEOFHOME.COM

SAUSAGE BREAKFAST BURRITOS

Burritos are a fun and filling way to serve up eggs and sausage and wake up taste buds.
—*Brenda Spann, Granger, IN*

TAKES: 20 min. • **MAKES:** 8 servings

1 lb. bulk pork sausage
1 small onion, chopped
½ green pepper, chopped
1 can (4 oz.) mushroom stems and pieces, drained
1 Tbsp. butter
6 large eggs, beaten
8 flour tortillas (8 in.), warmed
1 cup shredded cheddar cheese
 Salsa, optional

1. In a large skillet, brown sausage. Drain, reserving 2 Tbsp. drippings. Saute the onion, green pepper and mushrooms in drippings until tender.

2. In another skillet, melt butter over medium-high heat. Add eggs; cook and stir until set.

3. Divide sausage mixture among tortillas; top with eggs and cheese. Fold bottom of tortilla over filling and roll up. Serve with salsa if desired.

1 BURRITO: 429 cal., 25g fat (9g sat. fat), 188mg chol., 778mg sod., 30g carb. (1g sugars, 2g fiber), 19g pro.

HAWAIIAN WAFFLES

I created this waffle recipe to recapture the memorable tropical tastes we enjoyed while visiting Hawaii.
—*Darlene Brenden, Salem, OR*

TAKES: 30 min. • **MAKES:** 16 (4-in.) waffles

1 can (20 oz.) crushed pineapple, undrained
½ cup sugar
½ cup sweetened shredded coconut
½ cup light corn syrup
¼ cup pineapple juice

WAFFLES
2 cups all-purpose flour
4 tsp. baking powder
1 Tbsp. sugar
½ tsp. salt
2 large eggs, separated, room temperature
1 cup whole milk
¼ cup butter, melted
1 can (8 oz.) crushed pineapple, well drained
¼ cup sweetened shredded coconut
¼ cup chopped macadamia nuts
Additional chopped macadamia nuts, toasted, optional

1. In a large saucepan, combine the first 5 ingredients. Bring to a boil. Reduce heat. Simmer, uncovered, until sauce begins to thicken, 12-15 minutes; set aside.

2. In a large bowl, combine the flour, baking powder, sugar and salt. Combine egg yolks, milk and butter; stir into dry ingredients just until combined. Stir in pineapple, coconut and nuts. Beat egg whites until stiff peaks form; fold into batter (batter will be thick).

3. Preheat waffle maker. Fill and bake according to manufacturer's directions. Serve with pineapple sauce and additional nuts if desired.

2 WAFFLES: 446 cal., 14g fat (8g sat. fat), 73mg chol., 495mg sod., 76g carb. (43g sugars, 2g fiber), 7g pro.

🟤 GERMAN POTATO OMELET

This is an old German dish that was served to threshers and us kids when I was growing up. With a side of toast and jam, this flavorful omelet will make your family as happy as it made all of us.
—*Katherine Stallwood, Richland, WA*

TAKES: 30 min. • **MAKES:** 4 servings

2 **large potatoes, thinly sliced**
¼ **cup butter, divided**
½ **cup sliced green onions**
8 **large eggs**
¼ **cup 2% milk**
   Salt and pepper to taste

1. In a large skillet, cook potatoes in 2 Tbsp. butter for 15 minutes or until browned and tender. Sprinkle with onions; set aside and keep warm. In a large nonstick skillet, melt remaining butter over medium-high heat. Whisk the eggs and milk. Add egg mixture to skillet (mixture should set immediately at edges).

2. As eggs set, push cooked edges toward the center, letting uncooked portion flow underneath. When the eggs are set, spoon potato mixture on one side; fold other side over filling. Invert omelet onto a plate to serve. Cut into wedges and season as desired.

1 PIECE: 400 cal., 22g fat (11g sat. fat), 404mg chol., 253mg sod., 35g carb. (3g sugars, 4g fiber), 17g pro.

PUFFY APPLE OMELET

With all the eggs our chickens produce, I could make this omelet every day!
It's a festive-looking dish, but you could fix it anytime—including for a light supper.
—*Melissa Davenport, Campbell, MN*

TAKES: 30 min. • **MAKES:** 2 servings

3 Tbsp. all-purpose flour
¼ tsp. baking powder
⅛ tsp. salt, optional
2 large eggs, separated, room temperature
3 Tbsp. 2% milk
1 Tbsp. lemon juice
3 Tbsp. sugar

TOPPING

1 large apple, peeled if desired and thinly sliced
1 tsp. sugar
¼ tsp. ground cinnamon

1. Preheat oven to 375°. Mix flour, baking powder and, if desired, salt. In a small bowl, whisk together egg yolks, milk and lemon juice; stir into flour mixture.

2. In another bowl, beat egg whites on medium speed until foamy. Gradually add the sugar, 1 Tbsp. at a time, beating on high after each addition until stiff peaks form. Fold into flour mixture.

3. Pour into a 9-in. deep-dish pie plate coated with cooking spray. Arrange apple slices over top. Mix sugar and cinnamon; sprinkle over apple.

4. Bake, uncovered, until a knife inserted in the center comes out clean, 18-20 minutes. Serve immediately.

1 PIECE: 253 cal., 5g fat (2g sat. fat), 188mg chol., 142mg sod., 44g carb. (32g sugars, 2g fiber), 9g pro.

TEST KITCHEN TIP

Most puff pancakes are pretty lean, but satisfying even as breakfast for dinner. The filling often makes them unhealthy, but this puffy omelet recipe uses just a touch of sugar for sweetness.

CHORIZO & GRITS BREAKFAST BOWLS

Growing up, I bonded with my dad over chorizo and eggs. My fresh approach combines them with grits and black beans. Add a spoonful of pico de gallo.
—*Jenn Tidwell, Fair Oaks, CA*

TAKES: 30 min. • **MAKES:** 6 servings

2 tsp. olive oil
1 pkg. (12 oz.) fully cooked chorizo chicken sausages or flavor of choice, sliced
1 large zucchini, chopped
3 cups water
¾ cup quick-cooking grits
1 can (15 oz.) black beans, rinsed and drained
½ cup shredded cheddar cheese
6 large eggs
Optional: Pico de gallo and chopped fresh cilantro

TEST KITCHEN TIP

Pulses like black beans are part of the legume family and are a rich source of iron, which helps transport oxygen to muscles.

1. In a large skillet, heat oil over medium heat. Add the sausage; cook and stir until lightly browned, 2-3 minutes. Add zucchini; cook and stir until tender, 4-5 minutes longer. Remove from pan; keep warm.

2. Meanwhile, in a large saucepan, bring water to a boil. Slowly stir in grits. Reduce heat to medium-low; cook, covered, until thickened, stirring occasionally, about 5 minutes. Stir in the beans and cheese until blended. Remove from heat.

3. Wipe skillet clean; coat with cooking spray and place over medium heat. In batches, break 1 egg at a time into pan. Immediately reduce heat to low; cook until whites are completely set and yolks begin to thicken but are not hard, about 5 minutes.

4. To serve, divide the grits mixture among 6 bowls. Top with chorizo mixture, eggs and, if desired, pico de gallo and cilantro.

1 SERVING: 344 cal., 14g fat (5g sat. fat), 239mg chol., 636mg sod., 30g carb. (4g sugars, 4g fiber), 24g pro. *Diabetic exchanges:* 3 medium-fat meat, 2 starch.

BUTTERMILK CHOCOLATE CHIP PANCAKES

At our house, Saturday morning means pancakes for breakfast. I make the menu special by servings up stacks of these fluffy buttermilk treats studded with mini chips.
—*Julianne Johnson, Grove City, MN*

TAKES: 20 min. • **MAKES:** 16 pancakes

2 cups all-purpose flour
2 tsp. sugar
2 tsp. baking powder
1 tsp. baking soda
¼ tsp. salt
2 large eggs, room temperature, lightly beaten
2 cups buttermilk
¼ cup vegetable oil
⅔ cup miniature semisweet chocolate chips

1. In a bowl, combine the first 5 ingredients. Combine the eggs, buttermilk and oil; stir into dry ingredients just until moistened. Pour the batter by ¼ cupfuls onto a greased hot griddle.

2. Sprinkle each pancake with 2 tsp. chocolate chips. Turn when bubbles for on top of pancake; cook until second side is golden brown.

2 PANCAKES: 291 cal., 13g fat (4g sat. fat), 49mg chol., 487mg sod., 37g carb. (12g sugars, 2g fiber), 7g pro.

READER RAVE

"I made the batter the night before and put it in the fridge. It was perfect. My daughter loved them."
—QUEENLALISA, TASTEOFHOME.COM

⑤ BUFFET SCRAMBLED EGGS

These are my favorite scrambled eggs. The white sauce, flavored with chicken bouillon, keeps the eggs creamy and moist. It's a tasty twist on a morning mainstay.
—*Elsie Beachy, Plain City, OH*

TAKES: 20 min. • **MAKES:** 8 servings

8 **Tbsp. butter, divided**
¼ **cup all-purpose flour**
2 **cups whole milk**
4 **tsp. chicken bouillon granules**
16 **large eggs, lightly beaten**
   Optional: Minced fresh parsley, tarragon and chives

1. In a small saucepan, melt 2 Tbsp. butter. Stir in flour until smooth. Gradually add milk and bouillon granules. Bring to a boil; cook and stir for 2 minutes or until mixture is thickened. Set aside.

2. In a large skillet, melt remaining butter. Add the eggs; cook over medium heat until eggs begin to set, stirring occasionally. Stir in white sauce. Cook until the eggs are completely set. If desired, sprinkle with parsley, tarragon and chives.

¾ CUP: 304 cal., 24g fat (11g sat. fat), 464mg chol., 692mg sod., 7g carb. (4g sugars, 0 fiber), 15g pro.

POWER BERRY SMOOTHIE BOWL

Here's a nutrient-packed breakfast in a bowl. Not a fan of spinach? Don't worry, the berries and banana mask its flavor.
—*Christine Hair, Odessa, FL*

TAKES: 10 min. • **MAKES:** 3 servings

½ cup orange juice
½ cup pomegranate juice
1 container (6 oz.) mixed berry yogurt
1 cup frozen unsweetened strawberries
1 cup fresh baby spinach
½ medium ripe frozen banana, sliced
½ cup frozen unsweetened blueberries
2 Tbsp. ground flaxseed
Optional: Sliced fresh strawberries, fresh blueberries, flaxseed and granola

In a blender, combine the first 8 ingredients; cover and process for 30 seconds or until smooth. Pour into chilled bowls; top as desired. Serve immediately.

1 CUP: 172 cal., 3g fat (0 sat. fat), 3mg chol., 47mg sod., 35g carb. (28g sugars, 4g fiber), 5g pro.

READER RAVE

"Really liked this smoothie—did not have OJ and had kale from the garden, which was used as a substitute without any flavor change. I'm sure the OJ would have thinned it down, but I liked it as is."

—961 LEADER, TASTEOFHOME.COM

BACON & EGG SANDWICHES

I came across this unique grilled combo when I was digging in my mom's recipe box. The crisp bacon, hard-boiled eggs and crunchy green onions make these cozy sandwiches look impressive when company drops by for brunch. Best of all, they're a snap to assemble.
—*Ann Fuemmeler, Glasgow, MO*

TAKES: 20 min. • **MAKES:** 4 servings

½ cup sour cream
8 slices bread
4 green onions, chopped
4 slices American cheese
2 hard-boiled large eggs, cut into ¼-in. slices
8 cooked bacon strips
2 Tbsp. butter, softened

1. Spread sour cream over 4 bread slices; top with green onions, cheese, eggs, bacon and remaining bread. Spread outsides of sandwiches with butter.

2. Toast sandwiches until golden brown and cheese is melted, 2-3 minutes per side.

1 SANDWICH: 461 cal., 27g fat (13g sat. fat), 137mg chol., 887mg sod., 32g carb. (6g sugars, 2g fiber), 19g pro.

POWERHOUSE PROTEIN PARFAITS

Parfaits have marvelous taste and texture, but many are loaded with sugar and leave you hungry for more. Here's my protein-inspired option filled with cereal, fruit and nuts.
—*Jen Hubin, Minnetonka, MN*

TAKES: 15 min. • **MAKES:** 4 servings

3 cups plain Greek yogurt
⅓ cup honey
2 tsp. grated orange zest
2 cups Kashi Go Lean Crunch cereal
2 cups orange segments
2 cups fresh raspberries
¼ cup sliced almonds, toasted

In a bowl, mix yogurt, honey and orange zest until blended. Layer half the yogurt mixture, cereal, orange segments and raspberries among 4 parfait glasses. Repeat layers; sprinkle with almonds. Serve immediately.

1 PARFAIT: 518 cal., 22g fat (11g sat. fat), 45mg chol., 173mg sod., 75g carb. (50g sugars, 12g fiber), 15g pro.

TEST KITCHEN TIP
When most people think of yogurt, they think of single-serve containers for easy snacks and breakfasts, but yogurt can be so much more! Layered with fruit and cereal, it's easy to make a beautiful parfait like the one here. You can also use yogurt to make a tasty tzatziki sauce to serve with dinner or for a variety of delicious, creamy dips or dressings. Or use plain yogurt in place of sour cream on tacos, baked potatoes, soup, chili or other entrees.

SHEEPHERDER'S BREAKFAST

My sister-in-law always made this delicious dish when we were camping.
One-dish casseroles like this were a big help while I was raising my
nine children, and now I've passed the recipe on to them.
—*Pauletta Bushnell, Albany, OR*

. . . .

TAKES: 30 min. • **MAKES:** 8 servings

¾ lb. bacon strips, finely chopped
1 medium onion, chopped
1 pkg. (30 oz.) frozen shredded hash brown potatoes, thawed
8 large eggs
½ tsp. salt
¼ tsp. pepper
1 cup shredded cheddar cheese

1. In a large skillet, cook bacon and onion over medium heat until bacon is crisp. Drain, reserving ¼ cup drippings in pan.

2. Stir in the hash browns. Cook, uncovered, over medium heat until bottom is golden brown, about 10 minutes. Turn potatoes. With the back of a spoon, make 8 evenly spaced wells in the potato mixture. Break 1 egg into each well. Sprinkle with salt and pepper.

3. Cook, covered, on low until eggs are set and potatoes are tender, about 10 minutes. Sprinkle with cheese; let stand until cheese is melted.

1 SERVING: 354 cal., 22g fat (9g sat. fat), 222mg chol., 617mg sod., 22g carb. (2g sugars, 1g fiber), 17g pro.

MEATBALLS WITH
MARINARA SAUCE, 40

CHAPTER 2

FAVORITE APPS & SNACKS

Need an appetizer in a flash? Skip the standard bag of chips or can of nuts and go with one of these quick-to-fix party pleasers.

BACON CHEDDAR POTATO SKINS

You can't go wrong with a classic restaurant fave. My family often requests these crisp and hearty dressed-up skins.

—*Trish Perrin, Keizer, OR*

TAKES: 30 min. • **MAKES:** 8 servings

4   **large baking potatoes, baked**

3   **Tbsp. canola oil**

1   **Tbsp. grated Parmesan cheese**

½   **tsp. salt**

¼   **tsp. garlic powder**

¼   **tsp. paprika**

⅛   **tsp. pepper**

8   **bacon strips, cooked and crumbled**

1½   **cups shredded cheddar cheese**

½   **cup sour cream**

4   **green onions, sliced**

1. Preheat oven to 475°. Cut baking potatoes in half lengthwise; scoop out pulp, leaving a ¼-in. shell (save pulp for another use). Place potato skins on a greased baking sheet.

2. Combine oil with next 5 ingredients; brush over both sides of skins.

3. Bake until crisp, about 7 minutes on each side. Sprinkle bacon and cheddar cheese inside skins. Bake until cheese is melted, about 2 minutes longer. Top with sour cream and onions. Serve immediately.

1 POTATO SKIN: 350 cal., 19g fat (7g sat. fat), 33mg chol., 460mg sod., 34g carb. (2g sugars, 4g fiber), 12g pro.

DID YOU KNOW?

If potato skins have a hint of green, peel or cut off that section before eating. The green tint comes from high levels of solanine, which can be toxic when eaten in quantity. Although it is unlikely that enough solanine would be consumed to cause harm, it's best to be cautious and remove those parts.

51 SCARLET SIPPER

This sweet, tart and slightly fizzy drink is a favorite for gatherings at our church.
The bright color sets a festive tone, and the flavors blend seamlessly.
—*Amber Goolsby, Geneva, AL*

TAKES: 5 min. • **MAKES:** 12 servings (2¼ qt.)

4 cups cranberry-apple
  juice, chilled
1 cup orange juice, chilled
¼ cup lemon juice, chilled
1 liter ginger ale, chilled
  **Optional: Fresh
  cranberries, orange
  and lemon wedges**

In a pitcher, combine juices; stir in ginger ale. Serve over ice. If desired, garnish with cranberries, orange and lemon wedges.

¾ CUP: 91 cal., 0 fat (0 sat. fat), 0 chol., 8mg sod., 23g carb. (21g sugars, 0 fiber), 0 pro.

5i MEATBALLS WITH MARINARA SAUCE

Pack on the flavor with just a few easy ingredients. Enjoy these meatballs as a quick hot appetizer or serve them over your favorite hot pasta for a main dish.
—*Lauren Knoelke, Des Moines, IA*

. . . .

TAKES: 30 min. • **MAKES:** 20 servings

1   **pkg. (22 oz.) frozen fully cooked angus beef meatballs**
1½   **cups marinara sauce**
⅓   **cup chopped ripe olives**
½   **cup fresh basil leaves, torn**

1. Prepare meatballs according to package directions.

2. Meanwhile, in a saucepan, combine marinara sauce and olives; heat through. Add the meatballs and basil; heat through.

1 MEATBALL: 93 cal., 7g fat (3g sat. fat), 17mg chol., 301mg sod., 3g carb. (1g sugars, 1g fiber), 4g pro.

TEST KITCHEN TIP

Frozen meatballs are a great convenience item to have on hand as the possibilities are almost limitless. Fry them up in a pan and top your favorite pasta dish or toss them in a slow cooker with the sauce of your choosing for an easy appetizer.

HOT PIZZA DIP

You can assemble this effortless appetizer in a jiffy.
The pizza-flavored dip goes fast, so you may want to make two batches.
—*Stacie Morse, South Otselic, NY*

TAKES: 10 min. • **MAKES:** 24 servings (about 3 cups)

1 pkg. (8 oz.) cream cheese, softened

1 tsp. Italian seasoning

1 cup shredded part-skim mozzarella cheese

¾ cup grated Parmesan cheese

1 can (8 oz.) pizza sauce

2 Tbsp. chopped green pepper

2 Tbsp. thinly sliced green onion

Breadsticks or tortilla chips

1. In a bowl, beat cream cheese and Italian seasoning. Spread in an ungreased 9-in. microwave-safe pie plate.

2. Combine mozzarella and Parmesan cheeses; sprinkle half over the cream cheese. Top with the pizza sauce, remaining cheese mixture, green pepper and onion.

3. Microwave, uncovered, on high for 2-3 minutes or until cheese is almost melted, rotating a half-turn several times. Let stand for 1-2 minutes. Serve with breadsticks or tortilla chips.

2 TBSP.: 62 cal., 5g fat (3g sat. fat), 16mg chol., 131mg sod., 1g carb. (1g sugars, 0 fiber), 3g pro.

CALZONE PINWHEELS

These pretty bites take advantage of convenient refrigerator crescent rolls and they can be made ahead and popped in the oven right before company arrives. People love the cheesy, fresh taste—no one can eat just one!
—Lisa Smith, Bryan, OH

TAKES: 30 min. • **MAKES:** 16 appetizers

½ cup shredded part-skim mozzarella cheese

½ cup part-skim ricotta cheese

½ cup diced pepperoni

¼ cup grated Parmesan cheese

¼ cup chopped fresh mushrooms

¼ cup finely chopped green pepper

2 Tbsp. finely chopped onion

1 tsp. Italian seasoning

¼ tsp. salt

1 pkg. (8 oz.) refrigerated crescent rolls

1 jar (14 oz.) pizza sauce, warmed

1. Preheat oven to 375°. In a small bowl, mix the first 9 ingredients.

2. Unroll crescent dough and separate into 4 rectangles; press perforations to seal. Spread rectangles with cheese mixture to within ¼ in. of edges. Roll up jelly-roll style, starting with a short side; pinch seam to seal.

3. Using a serrated knife, cut each roll into 4 slices; place on a greased baking sheet, cut side down. Bake until golden brown, 12-15 minutes. Serve with warmed pizza sauce.

1 APPETIZER: 118 cal., 7g fat (3g sat. fat), 11mg chol., 383mg sod., 8g carb. (3g sugars, 0 fiber), 4g pro.

FOUR-TOMATO SALSA

The variety of tomatoes, onions and peppers is what makes this chunky salsa so good. Whenever I make a batch to take to a get-together, it's hard to keep my family from finishing it off first!
—*Connie Siese, Wayne, MI*

TAKES: 30 min. • **MAKES:** 56 servings (14 cups)

7   plum tomatoes, chopped
7   medium red tomatoes, chopped
3   medium yellow tomatoes, chopped
3   medium orange tomatoes, chopped
1   tsp. salt
2   Tbsp. lime juice
2   Tbsp. olive oil
1   medium white onion, chopped
1   medium red onion, chopped
2   green onions, chopped
½   cup each chopped green, sweet red, orange and yellow pepper
3   pepperoncini, chopped
⅓   cup mild pickled pepper rings, chopped
½   cup minced fresh parsley
2   Tbsp. minced fresh cilantro
1   Tbsp. dried chervil
    Tortilla chips

1. In a colander, combine the tomatoes and salt. Let drain for 10 minutes.

2. Transfer to a large bowl. Stir in the lime juice, oil, onions, peppers, parsley, cilantro and chervil. Serve with tortilla chips. Refrigerate leftovers for up to 1 week.

¼ CUP: 15 cal., 1g fat (0 sat. fat), 0 chol., 62mg sod., 2g carb. (1g sugars, 1g fiber), 0 pro. *Diabetic exchanges:* 1 free food.

TEST KITCHEN TIP

Look for pepperoncinis (pickled peppers) and pickled pepper rings in the pickle and olive aisle of your grocery store.

🄬 FRIED CHICKEN & PULLED PORK CORNBREAD POPPERS

If you're looking for a southern-inspired appetizer with a touch of heat,
start here. We love these on game day, but they'd be a hit at brunch, too.
—*Crystal Schlueter, Babbitt, MN*

TAKES: 25 min • **MAKES:** 2 dozen

2 oz. frozen popcorn
  chicken
1 pkg. (8½ oz.) cornbread/
  muffin mix
4 seeded jalapeno peppers
  or pickled jalapeno
  peppers, cut into 6 slices
  each
¼ cup refrigerated fully
  cooked barbecued pulled
  pork
½ cup maple syrup or honey
1 tsp. Sriracha chili sauce,
  optional

1. Preheat oven to 400°. Bake popcorn chicken according to package directions. When cool enough to handle, cut chicken into 12 pieces.

2. Meanwhile, prepare the cornbread mix according to package directions. Place a jalapeno slice in each of 24 foil-lined mini muffin cups. Fill each cup with 1 Tbsp. batter. Gently press a piece of popcorn chicken into the centers of half the cups. Spoon 1 tsp. pulled pork into the centers of remaining cups.

3. Bake until golden brown, about 12 minutes. Serve with maple syrup; if desired, whisk chili sauce into syrup.

NOTE: Wear disposable gloves when cutting hot peppers; the oils can burn skin. Avoid touching your face.

1 MINI MUFFIN: 74 cal., 2g fat (1g sat. fat), 10mg chol., 120mg sod., 13g carb. (7g sugars, 1g fiber), 2g pro.

OYSTER CHEESE APPETIZER LOG

Every winter, I make lots of cheese logs and freeze them for when I'm expecting company or need a special appetizer to take to a party or potluck. In this recipe, the blend of smoked oysters, chili powder, walnuts and cream cheese is out of this world. Serve with wheat, sesame or your favorite fancy crackers.

—William Tracy, Jerseyville, IL

TAKES: 20 min. • **MAKES:** 32 servings (2 logs)

3 pkg. (8 oz. each) cream cheese, softened
2 Tbsp. steak sauce
¼ cup Miracle Whip
1 garlic clove, peeled and minced, or 1 tsp. garlic powder
1 small onion, finely chopped
2 cans (3¾ oz. each) smoked oysters, well-drained and chopped
3 cups chopped pecans, divided
3 Tbsp. chili powder
Minced fresh parsley

In mixer bowl, combine the cheese, steak sauce, Miracle Whip, garlic and onion. Stir in oysters and 1 cup of pecans. Shape into two 9-in. logs. Roll logs in mixture of chili powder, remaining pecans and parsley.

2 TBSP.: 117 cal., 12g fat (2g sat. fat), 10mg chol., 62mg sod., 3g carb. (1g sugars, 1g fiber), 2g pro.

NUTTY STUFFED MUSHROOMS

Basil, Parmesan cheese and mushroom blend together well, while buttery pecans give these treats unexpected crunch. Our children, grandchildren and great-grandchildren always request them for family gatherings.
—*Mildred Eldred, Union City, MI*

TAKES: 30 min. • **MAKES:** 20 servings

20 large fresh mushrooms
3 Tbsp. butter
1 small onion, chopped
¼ cup dry bread crumbs
¼ cup finely chopped pecans
3 Tbsp. grated Parmesan cheese
¼ tsp. salt
¼ tsp. dried basil
   Dash cayenne pepper

1. Preheat oven to 400°. Remove the stems from the mushrooms; set caps aside. Finely chop stems. In a large skillet, heat butter over medium heat. Add the chopped mushrooms and onion; saute until liquid has evaporated, about 5 minutes. Remove from heat; set aside.

2. Meanwhile, combine remaining ingredients; add mushroom mixture. Stuff firmly into mushroom caps. Bake, uncovered, in a greased 15x10x1-in. baking pan until tender, 15-18 minutes. Serve warm.

1 STUFFED MUSHROOM: 44 cal., 3g fat (1g sat. fat), 5mg chol., 67mg sod., 3g carb. (0 sugars, 0 fiber), 2g pro.

SHRIMP TARTLETS

Mini tart shells filled with a cream cheese mixture and topped with seafood sauce and shrimp make the perfect bite-sized nosh. They're fantastic party appetizers, and several make a fast, light meal.
—*Gina Hutchison, Smithville, MO*

TAKES: 20 min. • **MAKES:** 2½ dozen

1 pkg. (8 oz.) cream cheese, softened
1½ tsp. Worcestershire sauce
1 to 2 tsp. grated onion
1 tsp. garlic salt
⅛ tsp. lemon juice
2 pkg. (1.9 oz. each) frozen miniature phyllo tart shells
½ cup seafood cocktail sauce
30 peeled and deveined cooked shrimp (31-40 per lb.), tails removed
Optional: Minced fresh parsley and lemon wedges

1. Beat first 5 ingredients until blended. Place tart shells on a serving plate. Fill with cream cheese mixture; top with cocktail sauce and shrimp.

2. Refrigerate until serving. If desired, sprinkle with parsley and serve with lemon wedges.

1 TARTLET: 61 cal., 4g fat (2g sat. fat), 23mg chol., 143mg sod., 4g carb. (1g sugars, 0 fiber), 3g pro.

⑤ CITRUS & WHITE GRAPE PARTY PUNCH

This light-colored punch is perfect for summertime parties or special occasions. Mix the first four ingredients ahead of time, refrigerate and add the soda right before serving.

—*Karen Ballance, Wolf Lake, IL*

TAKES: 5 min. • **MAKES:** 32 servings (4 qt.)

4 cups white grape juice, chilled

1 can (12 oz.) frozen lemonade concentrate, thawed

1 can (12 oz.) frozen orange juice concentrate, thawed

2 bottles (2 liters each) lemon-lime soda, chilled

Optional: Lemon slices, orange slices and green grapes

In a punch bowl, combine grape juice, lemonade concentrate and orange juice concentrate. Add soda; serve immediately. If desired, garnish with fruit.

½ CUP: 119 cal., 0 fat (0 sat. fat), 0 chol., 17mg sod., 30g carb. (26g sugars, 0 fiber), 0 pro.

TEST KITCHEN TIP

Chill all punch ingredients before mixing so that you don't have to dilute the punch with ice to get it cold. Or consider garnishing a cold punch with an ice ring (which lasts longer than ice cubes) made from punch ingredients instead of water.

SPINACH DEVILED EGGS

Spinach adds unexpected color and flavor to this tasty variation on deviled eggs. They're easy to make with leftover eggs and are an attractive addition to a party spread.
—*Dorothy Sander, Evansville, IN*

TAKES: 15 min. • **MAKES:** 2 dozen

12 hard-boiled large eggs
¼   cup mayonnaise
2   Tbsp. white vinegar
2   Tbsp. butter, softened
1   Tbsp. sugar
½   tsp. pepper
¼   tsp. salt
4   bacon strips, cooked and crumbled
½   cup frozen chopped spinach, thawed and squeezed dry

Cut eggs in half lengthwise. Remove yolks; set whites aside. In a small bowl, mash yolks. Add the mayonnaise, vinegar, butter, sugar, pepper and salt; mix well. Stir in bacon and spinach. Stuff or pipe filling into egg whites. Refrigerate until serving.

2 APPETIZERS: 146 cal., 12g fat (4g sat. fat), 221mg chol., 194mg sod., 2g carb. (2g sugars, 0 fiber), 7g pro.

SAUSAGE DIP

My warm sausage dip is a family-favorite on cool fall days.
Anyone with a hearty appetite will love this country-style appetizer.
—*Susie Wingert, Panama, IA*

TAKES: 30 min. • **MAKES:** 48 servings (6 cups)

1½ **lbs. bulk pork sausage**
2½ **cups chopped fresh mushrooms**
2 **medium green peppers, chopped**
1 **large tomato, seeded and chopped**
1 **medium red onion, chopped**
1½ **tsp. salt**
1 **tsp. pepper**
1 **tsp. garlic powder**
½ **tsp. onion powder**
2 **pkg. (8 oz. each) cream cheese, cubed**
1 **cup sour cream**
Tortilla chips

In a large skillet over medium heat, cook the sausage until no longer pink; drain. Add the next 8 ingredients; cook until the vegetables are tender. Reduce heat to low; add cream cheese and sour cream. Cook and stir until cheese is melted and well blended (do not boil). Serve warm with tortilla chips.

2 TBSP.: 59 cal., 5g fat (3g sat. fat), 13mg chol., 149mg sod., 1g carb. (1g sugars, 0 fiber), 2g pro.

ONE-POT SPINACH
BEEF SOUP, 68

CHAPTER 3

SOUPS, SALADS & SANDWICHES

These recipes prove that hot soups and hearty sandwiches make the ultimate combo. There's even a couple of fresh salads to round out these tasty mealtime match-ups.

FAJITAS IN PITAS

For a weekend lunch with company, we grill chicken and peppers to stuff inside pita pockets. The dressing doubles as a grilling sauce and a sandwich spread.
—*Clara Coulson Minney, Washington Court House, OH*

TAKES: 25 min. • **MAKES:** 4 servings

½ cup mayonnaise
1 green onion, chopped
4 tsp. Dijon mustard
¼ tsp. pepper
3 boneless skinless chicken breast halves (6 oz. each)
2 medium sweet red peppers, halved and seeded
2 medium green peppers, halved and seeded
8 pita pocket halves, warmed
8 lettuce leaves

1. In a small bowl, mix the mayonnaise, green onion, mustard and pepper; reserve ⅓ cup for assembling. Spread remaining mixture over chicken and peppers.

2. Grill chicken and peppers, covered, over medium heat or broil 4 in. from heat for 5-6 minutes on each side or until a thermometer inserted in chicken reads 165° and peppers are tender. Cut chicken into ½-in. slices; cut peppers into 1-in. slices.

3. Spread reserved mayonnaise mixture inside pita halves; fill with lettuce, chicken and peppers.

2 FILLED PITA HALVES: 515 cal., 24g fat (4g sat. fat), 72mg chol., 640mg sod., 39g carb. (5g sugars, 4g fiber), 33g pro.

PRESSURE-COOKER LENTIL PUMPKIN SOUP

A bounty of herbs and spices brighten up my hearty pumpkin soup.
It's the perfect warm-up for chilly days and nights.
—*Laura Magee, Houlton, WI*

TAKES: 25 min. • **MAKES:** 6 servings (2¼ qt.)

1 **lb. medium red potatoes (about 4 medium), cut into ½-in. pieces**

1 **can (15 oz.) canned pumpkin**

1 **cup dried lentils, rinsed**

1 **medium onion, chopped**

3 **garlic cloves, minced**

½ **tsp. ground ginger**

½ **tsp. pepper**

⅛ **tsp. salt**

2 **cans (14½ oz. each) vegetable broth**

1½ **cups water**

 Minced fresh cilantro, optional

In a 6-qt. electric pressure cooker, combine the first 10 ingredients. Lock the lid; close pressure-release valve. Adjust to pressure-cook on high for 12 minutes. Quick-release pressure. If desired, sprinkle servings with minced cilantro.

1½ CUPS: 210 cal., 1g fat (0 sat. fat), 0 chol., 463mg sod., 42g carb. (5g sugars, 7g fiber), 11g pro. *Diabetic exchanges:* 2½ starch, 1 lean meat.

ONE-POT SPINACH BEEF SOUP

My idea of a winning weeknight meal is this beefy soup that simmers in one big pot. Grate some Parmesan and pass the saltines.
—*Julie Davis, Jacksonville, FL*

TAKES: 30 min. • **MAKES:** 8 servings (2½ qt.)

1 lb. ground beef
3 garlic cloves, minced
2 cartons (32 oz. each) reduced-sodium beef broth
2 cans (14½ oz. each) diced tomatoes with green pepper, celery and onion, undrained
1 tsp. dried basil
½ tsp. pepper
½ tsp. dried oregano
¼ tsp. salt
3 cups uncooked bow tie pasta
4 cups fresh spinach, coarsely chopped
Grated Parmesan cheese

1. In a 6-qt. stockpot, cook beef and garlic over medium heat until beef is no longer pink, breaking up beef into crumbles, 6-8 minutes; drain. Stir in broth, tomatoes and seasonings; bring to a boil. Stir in pasta; return to a boil. Cook, uncovered, until pasta is tender, 7-9 minutes.

2. Stir in fresh spinach until wilted. Sprinkle servings with Parmesan cheese.

1⅓ CUPS: 258 cal., 7g fat (3g sat. fat), 40mg chol., 909mg sod., 30g carb. (8g sugars, 3g fiber), 17g pro.

READER RAVE

"We love a great soup recipe! This was a winner in our house. Sometimes we use the spicy Italian sausage instead of ground beef to give it more of a kick. Super dish."

—JGA2595176, TASTEOFHOME.COM

SPINACH QUESADILLAS

My family gave these cheesy quesadillas oohs and aahs. Remove the spinach from the heat as soon as it begins to wilt so it will retain a little bit of crunch.
—*Pam Kaiser, Mansfield, MO*

TAKES: 25 min. • **MAKES:** 4 servings

3 oz. fresh baby spinach (about 4 cups)
4 green onions, chopped
1 small tomato, chopped
2 Tbsp. lemon juice
1 tsp. ground cumin
¼ tsp. garlic powder
1 cup shredded reduced-fat Monterey Jack cheese or Mexican cheese blend
¼ cup reduced-fat ricotta cheese
6 flour tortillas (6 in.)
Reduced-fat sour cream, optional

1. In a large nonstick skillet, cook and stir the first 6 ingredients until spinach is wilted. Remove from heat; stir in cheeses.

2. Top half of each tortilla with spinach mixture; fold other half over filling. Place on a griddle coated with cooking spray; cook over medium heat until golden brown, 1-2 minutes per side. Cut quesadillas in half; if desired, serve with sour cream.

3 WEDGES: 281 cal., 12g fat (6g sat. fat), 24mg chol., 585mg sod., 30g carb. (3g sugars, 4g fiber), 14g pro. *Diabetic exchanges:* 2 starch, 1 medium-fat meat, 1 vegetable.

CHAMPION ROAST BEEF SANDWICHES

When I have time, I prepare a roast with this much-requested recipe in mind. But when I need a quick meal in a hurry, I use deli roast beef with delicious results.
—*Ann Eastman, Santa Monica, CA*

TAKES: 15 min. • **MAKES:** 4 servings

½ cup sour cream
1 Tbsp. onion soup mix
1 Tbsp. prepared horseradish, drained
⅛ tsp. pepper
8 slices rye or pumpernickel bread
½ lb. sliced roast beef
Lettuce leaves

In a small bowl, combine the first 4 ingredients. Spread 1 Tbsp. on each slice of bread. Top 4 slices of bread with roast beef and lettuce; cover with remaining bread.

1 SANDWICH: 318 cal., 11g fat (6g sat. fat), 60mg chol., 1401mg sod., 34g carb. (4g sugars, 4g fiber), 18g pro.

DID YOU KNOW?

Most of us have never eaten a spoonful of plain horseradish, but you've likely come across it spread between the layers of a good old-fashioned roast beef sandwich. Horseradish is the root of a perennial in the Brassica family, which also includes mustard, wasabi, broccoli and cabbage. Grated horseradish is spicy—it only takes a tablespoon to bring tears to your eyes—but unlike spicy peppers, the reaction is limited to a few moments.

PASTA FAGIOLI SOUP

My husband enjoys my version of this soup so much, he stopped ordering
it at restaurants. He'd rather savor the version we can have at home.
It's so easy to make, yet hearty enough to be a full dinner.
—*Brenda Thomas, Springfield, MO*

TAKES: 30 min. • **MAKES:** 5 servings

½ lb. Italian turkey sausage links, casings removed, crumbled
1 small onion, chopped
1½ tsp. canola oil
1 garlic clove, minced
2 cups water
1 can (15½ oz.) great northern beans, rinsed and drained
1 can (14½ oz.) diced tomatoes, undrained
1 can (14½ oz.) reduced-sodium chicken broth
¾ cup uncooked elbow macaroni
¼ tsp. pepper
1 cup fresh spinach leaves, cut as desired
5 tsp. shredded Parmesan cheese

1. In a large saucepan, cook the sausage over medium heat until no longer pink; drain, remove from pan and set aside. In the same pan, saute onion in oil until tender. Add garlic; saute 1 minute longer.

2. Add the water, beans, tomatoes, broth, macaroni and pepper; bring to a boil. Cook, uncovered, until macaroni is tender, 8-10 minutes.

3. Reduce heat to low; stir in sausage and spinach. Cook until spinach is wilted, 2-3 minutes. Garnish with cheese.

1⅓ CUPS: 228 cal., 7g fat (1g sat. fat), 29mg chol., 841mg sod., 27g carb. (4g sugars, 6g fiber), 16g pro. *Diabetic exchanges:* 1½ starch, 1 lean meat, 1 vegetable, ½ fat.

COBB SALAD WRAPS

These wraps are a fun riff on the classic Cobb salad. Avocado, bacon, blue cheese, tomato and a homemade dressing deliver the flavors I enjoy most.
—*Lynne Van Wagenen, Salt Lake City, UT*

TAKES: 15 min. • **MAKES:** 4 servings

2 cups cubed cooked chicken breast
½ cup chopped avocado
4 bacon strips, cooked and crumbled
1 celery rib, thinly sliced
1 green onion, sliced
2 Tbsp. chopped ripe olives
2 Tbsp. crumbled blue cheese
2 Tbsp. lemon juice
1 Tbsp. honey
1½ tsp. Dijon mustard
1 garlic clove, minced
¼ tsp. dill weed
¼ tsp. salt
⅛ tsp. pepper
1 Tbsp. olive oil
4 romaine leaves, torn
4 whole wheat tortillas (8 in.), warmed
1 medium tomato, chopped

1. In a small bowl, combine chicken, avocado, bacon, celery, onion, olives and cheese. In another small bowl, combine lemon juice, honey, mustard, garlic, dill weed, salt and pepper. Whisk in oil. Pour over the chicken mixture; toss to coat.

2. Place romaine on each tortilla; top with ⅔ cup chicken mixture. Sprinkle with tomato; roll up.

1 WRAP: 372 cal., 14g fat (3g sat. fat), 65mg chol., 607mg sod., 32g carb. (6g sugars, 6g fiber), 29g pro. *Diabetic exchanges:* 3 lean meat, 2 starch, 1 fat.

TURKEY-CRANBERRY MONTE CRISTO

Every year, my husband and I look forward to Thanksgiving leftovers just so we can make this. Once you try it, you'll agree this is the best turkey sandwich ever!
—*Cleo Gonske, Redding, CA*

TAKES: 30 min. • **MAKES:** 4 servings

8 slices egg bread
3 Tbsp. Dijon mustard
10 oz. thinly sliced cooked turkey
6 oz. smoked Gouda cheese, thinly sliced
½ cup whole-berry cranberry sauce
3 large eggs
⅓ cup 2% milk
¼ tsp. salt
¼ tsp. pepper
3 tsp. butter
3 tsp. canola oil

1. Preheat oven to 350°. Spread 4 slices of bread with Dijon mustard. Layer with the turkey and cheese. Spread remaining bread with cranberry sauce; place on cheese.

2. In a shallow bowl, whisk eggs, milk, salt and pepper. In a large skillet, heat 1½ tsp. each butter and oil over medium heat until butter is melted. Dip 2 sandwiches in egg mixture; add to skillet. Cook until golden brown, 2-3 minutes per side. Repeat with remaining butter, oil and sandwiches.

3. Transfer sandwiches to a baking sheet. Bake until cheese is melted, 4-5 minutes.

1 SANDWICH: 674 cal., 30g fat (13g sat. fat), 297mg chol., 1282mg sod., 56g carb. (12g sugars, 2g fiber), 44g pro.

SPICY BUFFALO CHICKEN WRAPS

This recipe has a real kick and is one of my husband's favorites. Ready in a flash, it's easily doubled and the closest thing to restaurant Buffalo wings I've ever tasted in a light version.
—*Jennifer Beck, Meridian, ID*

TAKES: 25 min. • **MAKES:** 2 servings

- ½ lb. boneless skinless chicken breast, cubed
- ½ tsp. canola oil
- 2 Tbsp. Louisiana-style hot sauce
- 1 cup shredded lettuce
- 2 flour tortillas (6 in.), warmed
- 2 tsp. reduced-fat ranch salad dressing
- 2 Tbsp. crumbled blue cheese

1. In a large nonstick skillet, cook chicken in oil over medium heat for 6 minutes; drain. Stir in hot sauce. Bring to a boil. Reduce heat; simmer, uncovered, for 3-5 minutes or until sauce is thickened and chicken is no longer pink.

2. Place lettuce on tortillas; drizzle with ranch dressing. Top with chicken mixture and blue cheese; roll up.

1 WRAP: 273 cal., 11g fat (3g sat. fat), 70mg chol., 453mg sod., 15g carb. (1g sugars, 1g fiber), 28g pro. *Diabetic exchanges:* 3 lean meat, 1½ fat, 1 starch.

READER RAVE

"This recipe is easy, healthy, budget-friendly and delicious! We used our favorite wing sauce and shredded cheddar cheese in place of the Louisiana hot sauce and the blue cheese."

—CMARIE_1124, TASTEOFHOME.COM

✵ CHEESY CHILI

My six grandchildren enjoy feasting on big bowls of this zesty chili.
It's so thick and creamy, you can even serve it as a dip at parties.
—*Codie Ray, Tallulah, LA*

TAKES: 25 min. • **MAKES:** 12 servings (about 3 qt.)

2 lbs. ground beef
2 medium onions, chopped
2 garlic cloves, minced
3 cans (10 oz. each) diced tomatoes and green chiles, undrained
1 can (28 oz.) diced tomatoes, undrained
2 cans (4 oz. each) chopped green chiles
½ tsp. pepper
2 lbs. Velveeta, cubed
Sour cream, sliced jalapeno pepper, chopped tomato, minced fresh cilantro, optional

1. In a large saucepan, cook the beef, onions and garlic until meat is no longer pink; drain. Stir in the tomatoes, chiles and pepper; bring to a boil.

2. Reduce heat; simmer, uncovered, for 10-15 minutes. Stir in cheese until melted. Serve immediately. If desired, top with sour cream, jalapenos, tomatoes and cilantro.

FREEZE: Allow chili to cool before freezing. To use, thaw in the refrigerator; heat in a saucepan or microwave. May be frozen for up to 3 months.

1 CUP: 396 cal., 25g fat (15g sat. fat), 85mg chol., 1166mg sod., 13g carb. (9g sugars, 2g fiber), 29g pro.

TURKEY & PASTA RANCH SALAD

Here's your new go-to recipe when your garden is bursting with fresh veggies. Chunks of tender turkey and classic ranch dressing make it appealing to kids and adults alike.

—*Julie Peterson, Crofton, MD*

TAKES: 25 min. • **MAKES:** 6 servings

- 2 **cups uncooked whole wheat spiral pasta (about 5 oz.)**
- 2 **medium sweet peppers, chopped**
- 1 **medium zucchini, thinly sliced**
- 1 **yellow summer squash, thinly sliced**
- ½ **cup finely chopped red onion**
- 2 **cups cubed cooked turkey or chicken**
- 3 **Tbsp. chopped fresh parsley**
- ½ **cup peppercorn ranch salad dressing**
- ¼ **tsp. salt**
- ¼ **cup shredded Parmesan cheese**

1. Cook pasta according to package directions. Drain and rinse with cold water; drain well.

2. Place pasta, vegetables, turkey and parsley in a large bowl; toss with dressing and salt. Sprinkle with cheese.

1⅔ CUPS: 256 cal., 11g fat (2g sat. fat), 50mg chol., 383mg sod., 20g carb. (4g sugars, 4g fiber), 19g pro. *Diabetic exchanges:* 3 lean meat, 1½ fat, 1 starch, 1 vegetable.

🟤 PRESSURE-COOKER CAROLINA-STYLE VINEGAR BBQ CHICKEN

I live in Georgia but enjoy the tangy, sweet and slightly spicy taste of Carolina vinegar chicken. Using a pressure cooker means I can get these sandwiches on the table fast!
—*Ramona Parris, Canton, GA*

TAKES: 25 min. • **MAKES:** 6 servings

2 cups water
1 cup white vinegar
¼ cup sugar
1 Tbsp. reduced-sodium chicken base
1 tsp. crushed red pepper flakes
¾ tsp. salt
1½ lbs. boneless skinless chicken breasts
6 whole wheat hamburger buns, split, optional

1. In a 6-qt. electric pressure cooker, mix the first 6 ingredients; add chicken. Lock lid and close the pressure-release valve. Adjust to pressure-cook on high for 5 minutes.

2. Allow pressure to naturally release for 8 minutes, then quick-release any remaining pressure.

3. Remove chicken and cool slightly. Reserve 1 cup cooking juices and discard remaining juices. Shred chicken with 2 forks. Combine with reserved juices. If desired, serve chicken mixture on buns.

½ CUP: 135 cal., 3g fat (1g sat. fat), 63mg chol., 228mg sod., 3g carb. (3g sugars, 0 fiber), 23g pro. *Diabetic exchanges:* 3 lean meat.

STRAWBERRY-CHICKEN SALAD WITH BUTTERED PECANS

Having lived in several states in the South, I developed a fondness
for pecans. I toss them into recipes for added flavor and crunch.
Fresh strawberries and rotisserie chicken round out this hearty salad.
—*Lisa Varner, El Paso, TX*

. . . .

TAKES: 15 min. • **MAKES:** 6 servings

2   **Tbsp. butter**
1   **cup pecan halves**
¼   **tsp. salt**
⅛   **tsp. pepper**
DRESSING
2   **Tbsp. balsamic vinegar**
2   **Tbsp. olive oil**
1   **Tbsp. sugar**
1   **Tbsp. orange juice**
⅛   **tsp. pepper**
SALAD
1   **pkg. (5 oz.) spring mix
    salad greens**
¾   **lb. sliced rotisserie
    chicken breast**
1   **cup sliced fresh
    strawberries**
1   **cup shredded Swiss
    cheese**
    Salad croutons, optional

1. In a large heavy skillet, melt butter. Add pecans; cook over medium heat until nuts are toasted, about 4 minutes. Stir in salt and pepper.

2. In a small bowl, whisk the dressing ingredients until blended. For salad, in a large bowl, combine the greens, chicken, strawberries and cheese. Drizzle with dressing and toss to coat. Serve with the buttered pecans and, if desired, croutons.

1 SERVING: 392 cal., 30g fat (8g sat. fat), 77mg chol., 210mg sod., 10g carb. (6g sugars, 3g fiber), 24g pro.

TEST KITCHEN TIP

Don't wash fresh strawberries until it's time to use them. Strawberries stay fresh longer if unwashed, with stems on, in a sealed glass jar in the refrigerator. Strawberries soak up moisture from washing, which can make them spoil in a hurry. It's not a long way from wet berries to moldy berries.

THYMED ZUCCHINI
SAUTE, 99

CHAPTER 4

SIDE DISHES

From old-fashioned biscuits to seasoned fresh veggies, any one of these will make the perfect accompaniment to your next meal.

HUSH PUPPIES

My mom is well known for her hush puppies. Her recipe is easy to prepare and gives tasty results. The chopped onion adds to the fantastic flavor.

—*Mary McGuire, Graham, NC*

TAKES: 25 min. • **MAKES:** 2 dozen

1 cup yellow cornmeal
¼ cup all-purpose flour
1½ tsp. baking powder
½ tsp. salt
1 large egg, lightly beaten
¾ cup 2% milk
1 small onion, finely chopped
Oil for deep-fat frying

1. In a large bowl, combine the cornmeal, flour, baking powder and salt. Whisk the egg, milk and onion; add to dry ingredients just until combined.

2. In a large cast-iron or electric skillet, heat oil to 365°. Drop batter by tablespoonfuls into oil. Fry until golden brown, 2-2½ minutes. Drain on paper towels. Serve hush puppies warm.

1 HUSH PUPPY: 55 cal., 3g fat (0 sat. fat), 9mg chol., 86mg sod., 7g carb. (1g sugars, 0 fiber), 1g pro.

TEST KITCHEN TIP

Hush puppies, deep-fried cornmeal balls typically served as a side dish with fish or seafood, are said to have originated in New Orleans in 1727. Deep frying is a quick process, so make sure you don't overcook or burn your hush puppies by leaving them in the oil for too long.

CREAMY BOW TIE PASTA

Add a little zip to your next meal with this saucy pasta dish. The classic Alfredo flavor makes it an excellent side with almost any meat or seafood.

—Kathy Kittell, Lenexa, KS

TAKES: 25 min. • **MAKES:** 2 servings

1 cup uncooked
  bow tie pasta
1½ tsp. butter
2¼ tsp. olive oil
1½ tsp. all-purpose flour
½ tsp. minced garlic
  Dash salt
  Dash dried basil
  Dash crushed
  red pepper flakes
3 Tbsp. 2% milk
2 Tbsp. chicken broth
1 Tbsp. water
2 Tbsp. shredded
  Parmesan cheese
1 Tbsp. sour cream

1. Cook bow tie pasta according to package directions. Meanwhile, in a small saucepan, melt butter. Stir in the oil, flour, garlic and seasonings until blended. Gradually add the milk, broth and water. Bring to a boil; cook and stir until slightly thickened, about 2 minutes.

2. Remove from the heat; stir in cheese and sour cream. Drain pasta; toss with sauce.

¾ CUP: 196 cal., 12g fat (5g sat. fat), 19mg chol., 252mg sod., 17g carb. (2g sugars, 1g fiber), 6g pro.

⑤ SEASONED OVEN FRIES

The next time you're craving fries, opt for these speedy, health-conscious wedges that bake in the oven. They're just as tasty as deep-fried versions and made with less mess.

—*Pat Fredericks, Oak Creek, WI*

. . . .

TAKES: 25 min. • **MAKES:** 2 servings

2 **medium baking potatoes**
2 **tsp. butter, melted**
2 **tsp. canola oil**
¼ **tsp. seasoned salt**
   Minced fresh parsley, optional

1. Cut each potato lengthwise in half; cut each piece into 4 wedges. In a large shallow dish, combine the butter, oil and seasoned salt. Add potatoes; turn to coat.

2. Place potatoes in a single layer on a baking sheet coated with cooking spray. Bake at 450° until tender, turning once, 20-25 minutes. If desired, sprinkle with minced parsley.

8 PIECE: 263 cal., 9g fat (3g sat. fat), 10mg chol., 242mg sod., 44g carb. (3g sugars, 4g fiber), 4g pro.

READER RAVE

"I've served this to a very picky group of kids I watch after school and they all love them with or without the potato skin on. From now on, I'll leave it on to save nutrients and time and the skin helps each fry to hold together just a little better after it's cooked. Cut them thin like fast-food fries and you'll save even more time in cooking. Best recipe for oven fries that I've ever tried."

—GALINTHEWOODS, TASTEOFHOME.COM

⑤ THYMED ZUCCHINI SAUTE

Simple and flavorful, this recipe is a tasty and healthy way to use up all those zucchini that are taking over your garden. It's ready in hardly any time!
—*Bobby Taylor, Ulster Park, NY*

TAKES: 15 min. • **MAKES:** 4 servings

1 Tbsp. olive oil
1 lb. medium zucchini, quartered lengthwise and halved
¼ cup finely chopped onion
½ vegetable bouillon cube, crushed
2 Tbsp. minced fresh parsley
1 tsp. minced fresh thyme or ¼ tsp. dried thyme

In a large skillet, heat oil over medium-high heat. Add zucchini, onion and bouillon; cook and stir 4-5 minutes or until zucchini is crisp-tender. Sprinkle with herbs.

NOTE: This recipe was prepared with Knorr vegetable bouillon.

¾ CUP: 53 cal., 4g fat (1g sat. fat), 0 chol., 135mg sod., 5g carb. (2g sugars, 2g fiber), 2g pro. *Diabetic exchanges:* 1 vegetable, ½ fat.

MASHED POTATOES WITH GARLIC-OLIVE OIL

Garlic mashed potatoes are high on our love list. To intensify the flavor, I combine garlic and olive oil in the food processor and drizzle it on top of the potatoes.

—*Emory Doty, Jasper, GA*

TAKES: 30 min. • **MAKES:** 12 servings

4 lbs. red potatoes, quartered
½ cup olive oil
2 garlic cloves
⅔ cup heavy whipping cream
¼ cup butter, softened
2 tsp. salt
½ tsp. pepper
⅔ to ¾ cup 2% milk
3 green onions, chopped
¾ cup grated Parmesan cheese, optional

1. Place potatoes in a Dutch oven; add water to cover. Bring to a boil. Reduce heat; cook, uncovered, until tender, 15-20 minutes. Meanwhile, place oil and garlic in a small food processor; process until blended.

2. Drain the potatoes; return to pan. Mash potatoes, gradually adding cream, butter, salt, pepper and enough milk to reach desired consistency. Stir in green onions. Serve with garlic-olive oil and, if desired, cheese.

NOTE: For food safety purposes, prepare garlic-olive oil just before serving; do not store leftover oil mixture.

¾ CUP MASHED POTATOES WITH 1 TBSP. CHEESE AND ABOUT 2 TSP. OIL MIXTURE: 299 cal., 20g fat (8g sat. fat), 31mg chol., 533mg sod., 26g carb. (3g sugars, 3g fiber), 5g pro.

CHIVE-CHEESE CORNBREAD

This cornbread goes well with any main dish, especially chili, pulled pork and fried chicken. The chives and sharp cheddar cheese give it a special flavor.
—*Sybil Eades, Gainesville, GA*

TAKES: 30 min. • **MAKES:** 15 servings

1 cup cornmeal
1 cup all-purpose flour
¼ cup sugar
4 tsp. baking powder
2 large eggs, room temperature
1 cup 2% milk
¼ cup butter, melted
1 cup shredded sharp cheddar cheese
3 Tbsp. minced chives

1. In a large bowl, combine cornmeal, flour, sugar and baking powder. In another bowl, whisk the eggs, milk and butter. Stir into dry ingredients just until moistened. Gently fold in cheese and chives.

2. Pour into a greased 13x9-in. baking pan. Bake at 400° until golden brown, about 18 minutes. Cut into strips; serve warm.

1 PIECE: 150 cal., 7g fat (4g sat. fat), 47mg chol., 200mg sod., 18g carb. (4g sugars, 1g fiber), 5g pro.

TEST KITCHEN TIP

Here are some hints for making the best cornbread.
• Before using cornmeal, make sure it's fresh. It should have a slightly sweet smell. Rancid cornmeal will smell stale and musty
• To avoid overmixing, stir the batter by hand just until moistened. Lumps in the batter are normal and desired.
• Don't let the mixed batter stand before baking. Have the oven preheated and the skillet or pan ready to go.
• Cornbread tastes best fresh from the oven. If that's not possible, serve it the same day it's made.
• If you like a more crusty cornbread, use a dark pan or skillet instead of one with a light finish.

🔟 FESTIVE CORN & BROCCOLI

This recipe is delicious and versatile. I often substitute a tablespoon
of minced fresh basil for the dried and two to three ears of sweet corn
(about a cup cut fresh from the cob) for the Mexicorn.
—*Lucile Throgmorton, Clovis, NM*

TAKES: 15 min. • **MAKES:** 5 servings

1   pkg. (16 oz.) frozen
    chopped broccoli, thawed
1   can (7 oz.) Mexicorn,
    drained
¼   cup butter, cubed
1   tsp. dried basil
½   tsp. salt
⅛   tsp. garlic powder
⅛   tsp. pepper

In a large cast-iron or other heavy skillet, combine the
broccoli, corn and butter; cook over medium heat until
butter is melted. Stir in the basil, salt, garlic powder
and pepper. Cover and cook until vegetables are tender,
8-10 minutes, stirring occasionally.

⅔ CUP: 135 cal., 9g fat (6g sat. fat), 24mg chol., 541mg sod.,
12g carb. (3g sugars, 4g fiber), 4g pro.

5i GRANDMA'S BISCUITS

Tender homemade biscuits add a warm and comforting touch to any meal.
My grandmother serves these alongside her seafood chowder.
—*Melissa Obernesser, Utica, NY*

TAKES: 25 min. • **MAKES:** 10 biscuits

2 cups all-purpose flour
3 tsp. baking powder
1 tsp. salt
⅓ cup shortening
⅔ cup 2% milk
1 large egg, lightly beaten

1. Preheat oven to 450°. In a large bowl, whisk flour, baking powder and salt. Cut in shortening until mixture resembles coarse crumbs. Add the milk and stir just until moistened.

2. Turn onto a lightly floured surface; knead gently 8-10 times. Pat dough into a 10x4-in. rectangle. Cut rectangle lengthwise in half; cut crosswise to make 10 squares.

3. Place 1 in. apart on an ungreased baking sheet; brush tops with egg. Bake until golden brown, 8-10 minutes. Serve warm.

1 BISCUIT: 165 cal., 7g fat (2g sat. fat), 20mg chol., 371mg sod., 20g carb. (1g sugars, 1g fiber), 4g pro.

READER RAVE

"Quick and easy and great with honey or butter and jam! My husband and I love these."
—ALLISON, TASTEOFHOME.COM

LEMON MUSHROOM ORZO

Sometimes I serve this side dish chilled and other times we enjoy it hot.
It has a pleasant tinge of lemon and a nice crunch from pecans.
—*Shelly Nelson, Akeley, MN*

TAKES: 25 min. • **MAKES:** 12 servings

1 pkg. (16 oz.) orzo pasta
3 Tbsp. olive oil, divided
¾ lb. sliced fresh mushrooms
¾ cup chopped pecans, toasted
½ cup minced fresh parsley
1 tsp. grated lemon zest
3 Tbsp. lemon juice
1 tsp. salt
½ tsp. pepper

1. Cook orzo according to package directions. Meanwhile, in a large skillet, heat 2 Tbsp. oil over medium-high heat. Add mushrooms; cook and stir until tender and lightly browned. Drain orzo.

2. In a large bowl, place orzo, mushroom mixture, pecans, parsley, lemon zest and juice, salt, pepper and remaining oil; toss to combine.

¾ CUP: 225 cal., 9g fat (1g sat. fat), 0 chol., 202mg sod., 31g carb. (2g sugars, 2g fiber), 6g pro. *Diabetic exchanges:* 2 starch, 1½ fat.

SAUCY SPROUTS & ORANGES

Expect compliments when you dish up this fun twist on Brussels sprouts. Citrus and mustard flavor the tasty sauce.

—*Carolyn Hannay, Antioch, TN*

TAKES: 30 min. • **MAKES:** 6 servings

3 medium navel oranges
1 lb. fresh Brussels sprouts, trimmed and halved
1 Tbsp. butter
2 tsp. cornstarch
2 Tbsp. honey mustard
¼ tsp. Chinese five-spice powder
2 Tbsp. slivered almonds, toasted

1. Finely grate zest of 1 orange; set zest aside. Cut that orange in half; squeeze juice into a 1-cup measuring cup. Add enough water to measure ½ cup; set aside. Peel and discard white membranes from remaining oranges; section them and set aside.

2. In a large saucepan, bring 1 in. water and Brussels sprouts to a boil. Cover and cook for 8-10 minutes or until crisp-tender.

3. Meanwhile, in a small saucepan, melt butter. Whisk cornstarch and reserved orange juice mixture until smooth; add to the butter. Stir in mustard and five-spice powder. Bring to a boil over medium heat; cook and stir for 1-2 minutes or until thickened and bubbly.

4. Drain sprouts; gently stir in orange sections. Transfer to a serving bowl; drizzle with the sauce. Sprinkle with almonds and grated orange zest.

¾ CUP: 97 cal., 4g fat (1g sat. fat), 5mg chol., 81mg sod., 15g carb. (8g sugars, 3g fiber), 4g pro. *Diabetic exchanges:* 1 vegetable, 1 fat, ½ fruit.

⑤ CORN FRITTER PATTIES

These five-ingredient fritters are a tasty and economical way to enjoy a southern staple without having to leave the house to go to your favorite seafood restaurant.
—*Megan Hamilton, Pineville, MO*

TAKES: 30 min. • **MAKES:** 4 servings

1   cup pancake mix
1   large egg, lightly beaten
¼   cup plus 2 Tbsp. 2% milk
1   can (7 oz.) whole kernel corn, drained
    Canola oil

1. In a small bowl, combine the pancake mix, egg and milk just until moistened. Stir in the corn.

2. In a cast-iron or electric skillet, heat ¼ in. oil to 375°. Drop batter by ¼ cupfuls into oil; press lightly to flatten. Cook until golden brown, about 2 minutes on each side.

2 FRITTERS : 228 cal., 11g fat (1g sat. fat), 48mg chol., 590mg sod., 26g carb. (5g sugars, 3g fiber), 6g pro.

🔵 CILANTRO GINGER CARROTS

Peppery-sweet ginger and cooling cilantro have starring roles in this colorful side of crisp-tender carrots. They go from pan to plate in minutes.
—Taste of Home *Test Kitchen*

TAKES: 15 min. • **MAKES:** 4 servings

1 Tbsp. butter
1 lb. fresh carrots, sliced diagonally
1½ tsp. minced fresh gingerroot
2 Tbsp. chopped fresh cilantro
½ tsp. salt
¼ tsp. pepper

In a large skillet, heat butter over medium-high heat. Add carrots; cook and stir 4-6 minutes or until crisp-tender. Add ginger; cook 1 minute longer. Stir in the cilantro, salt and pepper.

½ CUP: 73 cal., 3g fat (2g sat. fat), 8mg chol., 396mg sod., 11g carb. (5g sugars, 3g fiber), 1g pro. *Diabetic exchanges:* 1 vegetable, ½ fat.

TEST KITCHEN TIP

With its slightly sharp flavor, cilantro—also known as Chinese parsley—gives a distinctive taste to Mexican, Latin American and Asian dishes. Like other fresh herbs, cilantro should be used as soon as possible. Fresh herbs can be stored in the refrigerator up to 5-7 days. Wrap in a slightly damp paper towel and place in an airtight container. Wash just before using.

DAD'S COLA
BURGERS,141

CHAPTER 5

BEEF

Looking for a game-changing meal that's full of heartiness and vigor? These beefed-up recipes are a cut above the rest.

SKILLET NACHOS

My mom gave me a fundraiser cookbook, and the recipe for these skillet nachos has become a favorite. My family can't get enough. Add your go-to taco toppings such as sour cream, tomatoes, jalapeno and red onion.
—*Judy Hughes, Waverly, KS*

TAKES: 30 min. • **MAKES:** 6 servings

1 lb. ground beef
1 can (14½ oz.) diced tomatoes, undrained
1 cup fresh or frozen corn, thawed
¾ cup uncooked instant rice
½ cup water
1 envelope taco seasoning
½ tsp. salt
1 cup shredded Colby-Monterey Jack cheese
1 pkg. (16 oz.) tortilla chips
Optional toppings: Sour cream, sliced fresh jalapenos, shredded lettuce and lime wedges

1. In a large skillet, cook beef over medium heat until no longer pink, 6-8 minutes, breaking into crumbles; drain. Stir in tomatoes, corn, rice, water, taco seasoning and salt. Bring to a boil. Reduce heat; simmer, covered, for 8-10 minutes or until the rice is tender and mixture is slightly thickened.

2. Remove from heat; sprinkle with cheese. Let stand, covered, until cheese is melted, about 5 minutes. Divide tortilla chips among 6 plates; spoon beef mixture over chips. Serve with toppings as desired.

1 SERVING: 676 cal., 31g fat (10g sat. fat), 63mg chol., 1293mg sod., 74g carb. (4g sugars, 4g fiber), 25g pro.

51 BLUE CHEESE-CRUSTED SIRLOIN STEAKS

According to my wife, this smothered steak is my specialty.
I like to make it for her on Friday nights to say goodbye to a long week.
—*Michael Rouse, Minot, ND*

....

TAKES: 30 min. • **MAKES:** 4 servings

2 Tbsp. butter, divided
1 medium onion, chopped
⅓ cup crumbled blue cheese
2 Tbsp. soft bread crumbs
1 beef top sirloin steak
   (1 in. thick and 1½ lbs.)
¾ tsp. salt
½ tsp. pepper

1. Preheat the broiler. In a large broil-safe skillet, heat 1 Tbsp. butter over medium heat; saute onion until tender. Transfer to a bowl; stir in cheese and bread crumbs.

2. Cut the steak into 4 pieces; sprinkle with salt and pepper. In same pan, heat remaining butter over medium heat; cook steaks until desired doneness (for medium-rare, a thermometer should read 135°; medium, 140°), 4-5 minutes per side.

3. Spread onion mixture over steaks. Broil 4-6 in. from heat until lightly browned, 2-3 minutes.

NOTE: To make soft bread crumbs, tear bread into pieces and place in a food processor or blender. Cover and pulse until crumbs form. One slice of bread yields ½ to ¾ cup bread crumbs.

1 SERVING: 326 cal., 16g fat (8g sat. fat), 92mg chol., 726mg sod., 5g carb. (2g sugars, 1g fiber), 39g pro.

ROAST BEEF PASTA SKILLET

Leftover beef is the star in a skillet dinner that's perfect for two. Chopped tomato adds a burst of fresh flavor.
—Bill Hilbrich, St. Cloud, MN

TAKES: 20 min. • **MAKES:** 2 servings

1 cup uncooked spiral pasta
½ cup chopped onion
1 tsp. olive oil
1 tsp. butter
1 cup cubed cooked roast beef
1 tsp. pepper
½ cup chopped tomato
½ cup grated Parmesan cheese

Cook pasta according to package directions. Meanwhile, in a large skillet, saute onion in oil and butter until tender. Add roast beef and pepper; heat through. Drain pasta; add to beef mixture. Stir in tomato and cheese.

2 CUPS: 448 cal., 14g fat (6g sat. fat), 87mg chol., 358mg sod., 38g carb. (4g sugars, 3g fiber), 40g pro.

READER RAVE

"This is a very quick, easy-to-fix 'no-fuss' meal that's great with leftover roast or even beef luncheon meat! It's now part of my regular recipe rotation—a winner!"

—LLHEATH, TASTEOFHOME.COM

BROCCOLI BEEF BRAIDS

Each slice of this fast-to-fix, golden bread is like a hot sandwich packed with beef, broccoli and mozzarella.

—*Penny Lapp, North Royalton, OH*

TAKES: 30 min. • **MAKES:** 2 loaves (4 servings each)

1 lb. ground beef

½ cup chopped onion

3 cups frozen chopped broccoli

1 cup shredded part-skim mozzarella cheese

½ cup sour cream

¼ tsp. salt

¼ tsp. pepper

2 tubes (8 oz. each) refrigerated crescent rolls

1. Preheat oven to 350°. In a large skillet, cook beef and onion over medium heat 6-8 minutes or until beef is no longer pink, breaking up beef into crumbles; drain. Stir in the broccoli, mozzarella cheese, sour cream, salt and pepper; heat through.

2. Unroll 1 tube of the crescent dough onto a greased baking sheet; form into a 12x8-in. rectangle, pressing perforations to seal. Spoon half of the beef mixture lengthwise down center of rectangle.

3. On each long side, cut 1-in.-wide strips at an angle, about 3 in. into the center. Fold 1 strip from each side over filling and pinch ends together; repeat.

4. Repeat with remaining ingredients to make second braid. Bake 15-20 minutes or until golden brown.

2 PIECES: 396 cal., 23g fat (6g sat. fat), 48mg chol., 644mg sod., 29g carb. (8g sugars, 2g fiber), 20g pro.

❋ MEAT LOAF MUFFINS

Serve these tangy meat loaf muffins for dinner or slice them up for a take-along sandwich lunch. They're just as flavorful after freezing.
—*Cheryl Norwood, Canton, GA*

TAKES: 30 min. • **MAKES:** 6 servings

1   **large egg, lightly beaten**
½   **cup dry bread crumbs**
½   **cup finely chopped onion**
½   **cup finely chopped green pepper**
¼   **cup barbecue sauce**
1½ **lbs. lean ground beef (90% lean)**
3   **Tbsp. ketchup**
    Additional ketchup, optional

1. Preheat oven to 375°. Mix the first 5 ingredients. Add beef; mix lightly but thoroughly. Press about ⅓ cupful into each of 12 ungreased muffin cups.

2. Bake 15 minutes. Brush tops with 3 Tbsp. ketchup; bake until a thermometer reads 160°, 5-7 minutes. If desired, serve with additional ketchup.

FREEZE: Bake meat loaves without ketchup; cover and freeze on a waxed paper-lined baking sheet until firm. Transfer meat loaves to an airtight freezer container; return to freezer. To use, partially thaw in refrigerator overnight. Place meat loaves on a greased shallow baking pan. Spread with ketchup. Bake in a preheated 350° oven until heated through.

2 MINI MEAT LOAVES: 260 cal., 11g fat (4g sat. fat), 102mg chol., 350mg sod., 15g carb. (7g sugars, 1g fiber), 24g pro.

STEAK FAJITAS

Zesty salsa and tender strips of steak make these traditional fajitas extra special.
—*Rebecca Baird, Salt Lake City, UT*

TAKES: 30 min. • **MAKES:** 6 servings

2 large tomatoes,
 seeded and chopped
½ cup diced red onion
¼ cup lime juice
1 jalapeno pepper,
 seeded and minced
3 Tbsp. minced
 fresh cilantro
2 tsp. ground cumin, divided
¾ tsp. salt, divided
1 beef flank steak
 (about 1½ lbs.)
1 Tbsp. canola oil
1 large onion, halved
 and sliced
6 whole wheat tortillas
 (8 in.), warmed
 Optional: Sliced avocado
 and lime wedges

1. For salsa, place first 5 ingredients in a small bowl; stir in 1 tsp. cumin and ¼ tsp. salt. Let stand until serving.

2. Sprinkle steak with the remaining cumin and salt. Grill, covered, over medium heat or broil 4 in. from heat until meat reaches desired doneness (for medium-rare, a thermometer should read 135°), 6-8 minutes. Let stand 5 minutes.

3. Meanwhile, in a skillet, heat oil over medium-high heat; saute onion until crisp-tender. Slice steak thinly across the grain; serve in tortillas with onion and salsa. If desired, serve with avocado and lime wedges.

NOTE: Wear disposable gloves when cutting hot peppers; the oils can burn skin. Avoid touching your face.

1 FAJITA: 329 cal., 12g fat (4g sat. fat), 54mg chol., 498mg sod., 29g carb. (3g sugars, 5g fiber), 27g pro. *Diabetic exchanges:* 3 lean meat, 2 starch, ½ fat.

TEST KITCHEN TIP

To prevent the edges of flank steak from curling when grilling, score the surface with shallow diagonal cuts, making diamond shapes. This helps tenderize the meat as well.

QUICK CHILI MAC

This quick mac combines chili with one of my favorite pasta dishes. It's great to serve company or to take to potlucks. I occasionally add taco seasoning or use beanless chili and add black beans.

—*Lee Steinmetz, Lansing, MI*

TAKES: 20 min. • **MAKES:** 6 servings

1 cup uncooked elbow macaroni
1 lb. ground beef
1 small green pepper, chopped
1 small onion, chopped
2 cans (15 oz. each) chili with beans
1 can (11 oz.) whole kernel corn, drained
1 cup shredded cheddar cheese

1. Cook macaroni according to package directions; drain. Meanwhile, in a large skillet, cook and crumble beef with pepper and onion over medium heat until no longer pink, 5-7 minutes; drain.

2. Stir in chili, corn and macaroni; heat through. Sprinkle with cheese.

1⅓ CUPS: 422 cal., 21g fat (9g sat. fat), 89mg chol., 898mg sod., 27g carb. (6g sugars, 4g fiber), 30g pro.

STUFFED PEPPERS FOR FOUR

Truly a meal in one, this quick supper has it all: Veggies, meat, pasta and sauce, all packed into tender peppers. They will look so pretty on your table.
—Taste of Home *Test Kitchen*

TAKES: 30 min. • **MAKES:** 4 servings

½ cup uncooked orzo pasta

4 medium sweet peppers (any color)

¼ cup water

1 lb. ground beef

½ cup chopped onion

2 cups pasta sauce

1 cup frozen broccoli-cauliflower blend, thawed and chopped

½ cup grated Parmesan cheese, divided

1. Cook orzo according to package directions; drain. Cut and discard tops from peppers; remove seeds. Place in a 3-qt. round microwave-safe dish. Add water; microwave, covered, on high for 7-9 minutes or until the peppers are crisp-tender.

2. In a large skillet, cook and crumble beef with onion over medium heat until no longer pink, 5-7 minutes; drain. Stir in pasta sauce, vegetables, ¼ cup Parmesan cheese and orzo. Spoon into peppers. Sprinkle with the remaining cheese.

3. Microwave, uncovered, on high until heated through, 1-2 minutes.

1 STUFFED PEPPER: 448 cal., 18g fat (7g sat. fat), 79mg chol., 734mg sod., 41g carb. (15g sugars, 6g fiber), 30g pro.

GRILLED RIBEYES WITH GREEK RELISH

The classic Grecian flavors of olives, feta cheese and tomatoes are a surefire hit. Combine them to complement a perfectly grilled steak, and it's magic.

—Mary Lou Cook, Welches, OR

TAKES: 30 min. • **MAKES:** 4 servings

4 plum tomatoes, seeded and chopped
1 cup chopped red onion
⅔ cup pitted Greek olives
¼ cup minced fresh cilantro
¼ cup lemon juice, divided
2 Tbsp. olive oil
2 garlic cloves, minced
2 beef ribeye steaks (¾ lb. each)
1 cup crumbled feta cheese

1. For relish, combine tomatoes, onion, olives, cilantro, 2 Tbsp. lemon juice, oil and garlic.

2. Drizzle remaining lemon juice over steaks. Grill steaks, covered, over medium heat or broil 4 in. from heat for 5-7 minutes on each side or until meat reaches desired doneness (for medium-rare, a thermometer should read 135°; medium, 140°; medium-well, 145°). Let stand for 5 minutes before cutting steaks in half. Serve with relish and cheese.

4 OZ. COOKED BEEF WITH ⅔ CUP RELISH AND ¼ CUP CHEESE: 597 cal., 44g fat (16g sat. fat), 115mg chol., 723mg sod., 11g carb. (4g sugars, 3g fiber), 37g pro.

ZUCCHINI BEEF SKILLET

Here's speedy summer recipe that uses up those abundant garden goodies: Zucchini, tomatoes and green peppers. Ground beef makes it extra hearty.
—*Becky Calder, Kingston, MO*

TAKES: 30 min. • **MAKES:** 4 servings

1 lb. ground beef
1 medium onion, chopped
1 small green pepper, chopped
2 tsp. chili powder
¾ tsp. salt
¼ tsp. pepper
3 medium zucchini, cut into ¾-in. cubes
2 large tomatoes, chopped
¼ cup water
1 cup uncooked instant rice
1 cup shredded cheddar cheese

1. In a large skillet, cook and crumble the beef with onion and pepper over medium-high 5-7 minutes heat or until no longer pink; drain.

2. Stir in seasonings, vegetables, water and rice; bring to a boil. Reduce heat; simmer, covered, until rice is tender, 10-15 minutes. Sprinkle with cheese. Remove from heat; let stand until cheese is melted.

2 CUPS: 470 cal., 24g fat (11g sat. fat), 98mg chol., 749mg sod., 33g carb. (8g sugars, 4g fiber), 32g pro.

TEST KITCHEN TIP

Handle zucchini carefully; they're thin-skinned and easily damaged. To pick the freshest zucchini, look for a firm heavy squash with a moist stem end and a shiny skin. Smaller squash are generally sweeter and more tender than the larger ones. One medium (⅓ pound) zucchini yields about 2 cups of sliced or 1½ cups of shredded zucchini. Store zucchini in a plastic bag in the refrigerator crisper for 4 to 5 days. Do not wash until ready to use.

HEARTY VEGETABLE BEEF RAGU

This recipe is healthy yet satisfying, quick yet delicious. I can have a hot meal on the table in under 30 minutes, and it's one that my children will gobble up! If you are not fond of kale, stir in baby spinach or chopped broccoli instead.
—*Kim Van Dunk, Caldwell, NJ*

TAKES: 30 min. • **MAKES:** 8 servings

- 4 **cups uncooked whole wheat spiral pasta**
- 1 **lb. lean ground beef (90% lean)**
- 1 **large onion, chopped**
- 3 **garlic cloves, minced**
- 2 **cans (14½ oz. each) Italian diced tomatoes, undrained**
- 1 **jar (24 oz.) meatless spaghetti sauce**
- 2 **cups finely chopped fresh kale**
- 1 **pkg. (9 oz.) frozen peas, thawed**
- ¾ **tsp. garlic powder**
- ¼ **tsp. pepper**
  Grated Parmesan cheese, optional

1. Cook pasta according to package directions; drain. Meanwhile, in a Dutch oven, cook beef, onion and garlic over medium heat until beef is no longer pink, breaking up beef into crumbles, 6-8 minutes; drain.

2. Stir in the tomatoes, spaghetti sauce, kale, peas, garlic powder and pepper. Bring to a boil. Reduce heat; simmer, uncovered, until kale is tender, 8-10 minutes. Stir pasta into sauce. If desired, serve with cheese.

1½ CUPS: 302 cal., 5g fat (2g sat. fat), 35mg chol., 837mg sod., 43g carb. (15g sugars, 7g fiber), 20g pro. *Diabetic exchanges:* 2 starch, 2 lean meat, 2 vegetable.

READER RAVE

"A big hit with our teenage daughters. Easy to prepare and very tasty. Loved how it incorporated kale. For a recipe that's less of a ragu, omit the spaghetti sauce."

—NH-RESCUEE, TASTEOFHOME.COM

DAD'S COLA BURGERS

Before you hand out the drinks, save a little soda to make these delectable burgers. Cola, used in the meat mixture and brushed on during cooking, sparks the flavor and takes these to a whole new level.
—*Emily Nelson, Green Bay, WI*

TAKES: 25 min. • **MAKES:** 6 servings

½ cup crushed saltines (about 15 crackers)
½ cup (nondiet) cola, divided
6 Tbsp. French salad dressing, divided
1 large egg
2 Tbsp. grated Parmesan cheese
½ tsp. salt, divided
1½ lbs. lean ground beef (90% lean)
6 hamburger buns, split
Optional toppings: Lettuce leaves and tomato and red onion slices

1. Combine the saltine crumbs, ¼ cup cola, 3 Tbsp. salad dressing, egg, Parmesan cheese and ¼ tsp. salt. Add beef; mix well. Shape into six ¾-in.-thick patties (the mixture will be moist); sprinkle with remaining salt. Combine remaining cola and salad dressing.

2. Grill patties, covered, over medium heat 3 minutes per side. Brush with cola mixture. Grill, brushing and turning occasionally, 3-4 minutes longer or until a thermometer reads 160°. Serve on buns; if desired, top with lettuce, tomato and onion.

1 BURGER: 419 cal., 20g fat (6g sat. fat), 103mg chol., 698mg sod., 30g carb. (7g sugars, 1g fiber), 28g pro.

❄ EASY BEEF PIES

We make a lot of French dips and always have leftover roast beef—I put it to good use in these pies. Use any veggies you like. They're extra awesome drenched in cheese sauce.
—*Jennie Weber, Palmer, AK*

....

TAKES: 30 min. • **MAKES:** 4 servings

1   **pkg. (15 oz.) refrigerated beef roast au jus**
1   **Tbsp. canola oil**
¼   **cup finely chopped onion**
¼   **cup finely chopped green pepper**
1   **garlic clove, minced**
2   **sheets refrigerated pie crust**
1   **cup shredded Mexican cheese blend**
   Salsa con queso dip, optional

1. Preheat oven to 425°. Drain beef, reserving ¼ cup juices; shred meat with 2 forks. In a large skillet, heat oil over medium-high heat. Add onion and pepper; cook and stir 1-2 minutes or until tender. Add the garlic; cook 30 seconds longer. Remove from heat; stir in beef and reserved juices.

2. Unroll 1 pie crust; cut in half. Layer ¼ cup shredded cheese and about ⅓ cup beef mixture over half of each crust to within ½ in. of edge. Fold crust over filling; press edges with a fork to seal. Place on a greased baking sheet. Repeat with remaining crust and filling.

3. Bake 15-18 minutes or until golden brown. If desired, serve with queso dip.

FREEZE: Freeze cooled pies in a freezer container. To use, reheat pies on a greased baking sheet in a preheated 350° oven until heated through.

1 PIE: 752 cal., 46g fat (19g sat. fat), 108mg chol., 921mg sod., 53g carb. (7g sugars, 0 fiber), 31g pro.

CHICKEN WITH PEACH-CUCUMBER SALSA, 169

CHAPTER 6

POULTRY

There's nothing as mouthwatering, versatile and economical as poultry. Turn to one of these chicken or turkey recipes for a classic meal that's sure to please the whole family.

CHICKEN VEGGIE PACKETS

People think I went to a lot of trouble when I serve these packets. Individual aluminum foil pouches hold the juices during baking to keep the herbed chicken moist and tender. It saves time and makes cleanup a breeze.
—*Edna Shaffer, Beulah, MI*

TAKES: 30 min. • **MAKES:** 4 servings

4 boneless skinless chicken breast halves (4 oz. each)
½ lb. sliced fresh mushrooms
1½ cups fresh baby carrots
1 cup pearl onions
½ cup julienned sweet red pepper
¼ tsp. pepper
3 tsp. minced fresh thyme
½ tsp. salt, optional
Lemon wedges, optional

1. Flatten chicken breasts to ½-in. thickness; place each on a piece of heavy-duty foil (about 12-in. square). Layer the mushrooms, carrots, onions and red pepper over chicken; sprinkle with pepper, thyme and salt if desired.

2. Fold foil around chicken and vegetables and seal tightly. Place on a rimmed baking sheet. Bake at 375° for 30 minutes or until chicken juices run clear. If desired, serve with lemon wedges.

1 SERVING: 175 cal., 3g fat (1g sat. fat), 63mg chol., 100mg sod., 11g carb. (6g sugars, 2g fiber), 25g pro. *Diabetic exchanges:* 3 lean meat, 2 vegetable.

TEST KITCHEN TIP

Be careful when opening the foil packets as they will be full of steam. Pierce a small hole into the packet to release the steam if you know everything is cooked, or carefully unfold the foil using tongs to protect your hands.

BAVARIAN APPLE-SAUSAGE HASH

In the cooler months, nothing is as comforting as a hearty hash, and this one reflects my German roots. Enjoy it for dinner or as a brunch entree over cheddar grits or topped with a fried egg.
—*Crystal Schlueter, Babbitt, MN*

TAKES: 30 min. • **MAKES:** 4 servings

2 Tbsp. canola oil
½ cup chopped onion
4 fully cooked apple chicken sausages or flavor of your choice, sliced
1½ cups thinly sliced Brussels sprouts
1 large tart apple, peeled and chopped
1 tsp. caraway seeds
¼ tsp. salt
⅛ tsp. pepper
2 Tbsp. finely chopped walnuts
1 Tbsp. brown sugar
1 Tbsp. whole grain mustard
1 Tbsp. cider vinegar

1. In a large skillet, heat oil over medium-high heat; saute onion until tender, 1-2 minutes. Add sausages, Brussels sprouts, apple and seasonings; saute until lightly browned, 6-8 minutes.

2. Stir in walnuts, brown sugar, mustard and vinegar; cook and stir 2 minutes.

1 CUP: 310 cal., 17g fat (3g sat. fat), 60mg chol., 715mg sod., 25g carb. (19g sugars, 3g fiber), 16g pro.

TEX-MEX CHICKEN STRIPS

I was looking for a way to amp up the flavor of regular chicken strips
so I crushed some leftover corn chips to create a crispy, flavorful coating.
—*Cyndy Gerken, Naples, FL*

TAKES: 30 min. • **MAKES:** 4 servings

½ cup finely crushed
   corn chips

¼ cup panko (Japanese)
   bread crumbs

¼ cup dry bread crumbs

¼ cup finely shredded
   Mexican cheese blend

5 tsp. taco seasoning
   Dash cayenne pepper

¼ cup butter, melted

1 lb. chicken tenderloins

Preheat oven to 400°. In a shallow bowl mix the first
6 ingredients. Place butter in a separate shallow bowl.
Dip chicken in butter, then roll in crumb mixture to coat;
press to adhere. Place chicken on a foil-lined 15x10x1-in.
baking pan. Bake until a thermometer inserted into the
chicken reads 165°, about 15 minutes, turning halfway
through the cooking time.

3 OZ. COOKED CHICKEN: 258 cal., 14g fat (7g sat. fat), 85mg
chol., 351mg sod., 7g carb. (0 sugars, 0 fiber), 28g pro.

TEST KITCHEN TIP

The zesty seasoning on these chicken strips makes
them perfect for chopping into pieces and tossing over
a taco salad. If you like to dip your strips, try these with
salsa, guacamole, sour cream or ranch dressing.

SIMPLE SAUSAGE PASTA TOSS

For a flash of tasty inspiration, grab a skillet and stir up turkey sausage with tomatoes, garlic and olives. Toss everything with spaghetti, and sprinkle with Parmesan.
—Taste of Home *Test Kitchen*

TAKES: 25 min. • **MAKES:** 5 servings

8 oz. uncooked multigrain spaghetti

¼ cup seasoned bread crumbs

1 tsp. olive oil

¾ lb. Italian turkey sausage links, cut into ½-in. slices

1 garlic clove, minced

2 cans (14½ oz. each) no-salt-added diced tomatoes, undrained

1 can (2¼ oz.) sliced ripe olives, drained

1. Cook spaghetti according to package directions; drain. Meanwhile, in a large skillet, toss bread crumbs with oil; cook and stir over medium heat until toasted. Remove from pan.

2. Add sausage to same pan; cook and stir over medium heat until no longer pink. Add garlic; cook 30-60 seconds longer. Stir in tomatoes and olives; heat through. Add spaghetti and toss to combine. Sprinkle with toasted bread crumbs before serving.

1⅔ CUPS: 340 cal., 10g fat (2g sat. fat), 41mg chol., 689mg sod., 44g carb. (6g sugars, 6g fiber), 21g pro. *Diabetic exchanges:* 3 lean meat, 2 starch, 1 vegetable, ½ fat.

TURKEY & BROCCOLI PASTRY BRAID

This meal in one is an easy way to get kids—and adults—to eat broccoli.
The puff pastry that wraps up turkey, cheese and veggies is pure, flaky goodness.
—*Jenelle Fender, Steinbach, MB*

TAKES: 30 min. • **MAKES:** 4 servings

1 cup finely chopped cooked turkey (about 5 oz.)
½ cup finely chopped fresh broccoli
½ cup finely chopped sweet red pepper
½ cup shredded cheddar cheese
¼ cup Miracle Whip
¼ tsp. dill weed
1 sheet frozen puff pastry, thawed

1. Preheat oven to 400°. For filling, mix first 6 ingredients.

2. Unfold pastry onto a lightly floured surface; roll into a 15x10-in. rectangle. Transfer to a baking sheet. Spoon filling down center third of rectangle. On each long side, cut 8 strips about 3 in. into the center. Starting at an end, fold alternating strips over filling, pinching ends to join.

3. Bake until golden brown and filling is heated through, 20-25 minutes.

1 PIECE: 463 cal., 26g fat (7g sat. fat), 50mg chol., 435mg sod., 38g carb. (2g sugars, 5g fiber), 18g pro.

TEST KITCHEN TIP

After rolling out the puff pastry, loosely roll the dough around the rolling pin to easily lift and transfer it to a baking sheet. For a more finished look, brush the pastry with an egg wash before baking. To make egg wash, simply whisk 1 egg with 1 Tbsp. water.

⑤ ARTICHOKE CHICKEN PESTO PIZZA

Make pizza night an upscale affair with this fun twist on the traditional pie.
A prebaked crust and prepared pesto keep things quick and easy.
—*Trisha Kruse, Eagle, ID*

TAKES: 15 min. • **MAKES:** 8 servings

1   prebaked 12-in. pizza crust
½   cup prepared pesto
2   cups cubed cooked chicken breast
2   jars (6½ oz. each) marinated artichoke hearts, drained
2   cups shredded part-skim mozzarella cheese
    Grated Parmesan cheese and minced fresh basil, optional

Preheat oven to 425°. Place crust on an ungreased 12-in. pizza pan. Spread with pesto. Arrange chicken and artichokes over top; sprinkle with cheese. Bake until golden brown, 10-12 minutes. If desired, top with Parmesan cheese and minced fresh basil.

1 SLICE: 381 cal., 20g fat (6g sat. fat), 45mg chol., 880mg sod., 28g carb. (2g sugars, 4g fiber), 23g pro.

READER RAVE

"Fantastic recipe. So easy to put together and yummy. The best is I always have the ingredients ready. I buy the ready-made pesto from our market's salad bar."

—FERRYAL, TASTEOFHOME.COM

SKILLET CHICKEN FAJITAS

Fresh flavor with a flair describes this go-to recipe. Fajitas are just right for hot summer evenings when you want to serve something especially tasty, yet keep cooking to a minimum. Try topping them with sour cream, guacamole or both. My family loves them!

—Lindsay St. John, Plainfield, IN

. . . .

TAKES: 30 min. • **MAKES:** 6 servings

¼ cup lime juice
1 garlic clove, minced
1 tsp. chili powder
½ tsp. salt
½ tsp. ground cumin
2 Tbsp. olive oil, divided
1½ lbs. boneless skinless chicken breasts, cut into strips
1 medium onion, cut into thin wedges
½ medium sweet red pepper, cut into strips
½ medium yellow pepper, cut into strips
½ medium green pepper, cut into strips
½ cup salsa
12 flour tortillas (8 in.), warmed
1½ cups shredded cheddar cheese or Monterey Jack cheese

1. Mix first 5 ingredients and 1 Tbsp. oil. Add chicken; toss to coat. Let stand 15 minutes.

2. In a large nonstick skillet, heat remaining oil over medium-high heat; saute the onion and peppers until crisp-tender, 3-4 minutes. Remove from pan.

3. In same skillet, saute chicken mixture until no longer pink, 3-4 minutes. Stir in salsa and pepper mixture; heat through. Serve in tortillas. Sprinkle with cheese.

1 SERVING: 621 cal., 24g fat (8g sat. fat), 91mg chol., 999mg sod., 61g carb. (3g sugars, 4g fiber), 38g pro.

SPICY CHICKEN & BACON MAC

I've been working to perfect a creamy, spicy mac and cheese for years.
After adding smoky bacon, chicken, jalapenos and spicy cheese, this is the ultimate!
I use rotisserie chicken and precooked bacon when I'm pressed for time.
—Sarah Gilbert, Aloha, OR

TAKES: 30 min. • **MAKES:** 6 servings

1½ **cups uncooked cavatappi pasta or elbow macaroni**
3 **Tbsp. butter**
3 **Tbsp. all-purpose flour**
1½ **cups heavy whipping cream**
½ **cup 2% milk**
1 **tsp. Cajun seasoning**
¼ **tsp. salt**
¼ **tsp. pepper**
2 **cups shredded pepper jack cheese**
2 **cups shredded cooked chicken**
6 **bacon strips, cooked and crumbled**
1 **jalapeno pepper, seeded and chopped**
1 **cup crushed kettle-cooked potato chips or panko (Japanese) bread crumbs**

1. Cook pasta according to package directions for al dente; drain. Preheat broiler.

2. In a 10-in. cast-iron or other ovenproof skillet, heat butter over medium heat. Stir in flour until blended; cook and stir until lightly browned, 1-2 minutes (do not burn). Gradually whisk in cream, milk, Cajun seasoning, salt and pepper. Bring to a boil, stirring constantly. Reduce heat; cook and stir until thickened, about 5 minutes. Stir in cheese until melted. Add the pasta, chicken, bacon and jalapeno; cook and stir until heated through. Sprinkle chips over top.

3. Broil 3-4 in. from heat until chips are browned, about 30 seconds.

1 CUP: 673 cal., 50g fat (28g sat. fat), 175mg chol., 705mg sod., 26g carb. (3g sugars, 1g fiber), 32g pro.

TEST KITCHEN TIP

If your family's tastes lean toward spicy, toss in more chopped jalapeno pepper and/or an extra sprinkle of Cajun seasoning.

FETA-DILL CHICKEN BURGERS

I found fresh ground chicken at the butcher and gave it a whirl on our new grill. The result is these saucy burgers. Everybody went nuts—including my sister-in-law, an amazing cook!
—*Wendy Boughton, Victoria, BC*

TAKES: 25 min. • **MAKES:** 4 servings

1   **large egg, lightly beaten**
1   **large shallot, minced**
2   **Tbsp. crushed Ritz crackers**
2   **Tbsp. minced fresh dill**
3   **garlic cloves, minced**
¼   **tsp. salt**
¼   **tsp. pepper**
1   **lb. ground chicken**
½   **cup finely crumbled feta cheese**
2   **Tbsp. canola oil**
4   **hamburger buns, split**
    Refrigerated tzatziki sauce and sliced tomato, optional

1. Combine first 7 ingredients. Add chicken; mix lightly but thoroughly. Gently stir in cheese.

2. Shape into four ½-in. thick patties (mixture will be soft). Brush patties with oil. Grill, covered, over medium heat until a thermometer reads 165°, 5-6 minutes per side. Serve on buns. If desired, top with tzatziki sauce and sliced tomato.

1 BURGER: 414 cal., 22g fat (5g sat. fat), 129mg chol., 608mg sod., 27g carb. (4g sugars, 2g fiber), 27g pro.

⑤ BREADED TURKEY BREASTS

Turkey isn't just for Thanksgiving. Try these cutlets seasoned with Parmesan cheese and Italian herbs for a comforting weeknight dinner. The thin slices take only a few minutes on the stovetop, so be careful not to overcook them.
—*Rhonda Knight, Hecker, IL*

TAKES: 20 min. • **MAKES:** 4 servings

1 cup dry bread crumbs
¼ cup grated
   Parmesan cheese
2 tsp. Italian seasoning
¾ cup 2% milk
8 turkey breast cutlets
   (2 oz. each)
¼ cup olive oil

1. In a shallow bowl, combine bread crumbs, Parmesan cheese and Italian seasoning. Pour milk into another shallow bowl. Dip turkey in milk, then roll in crumbs.

2. In a large skillet, cook turkey in oil over medium heat for 4-5 minutes on each side or until juices run clear. Drain on paper towels.

2 CUTLETS: 364 cal., 18g fat (4g sat. fat), 73mg chol., 372mg sod., 16g carb. (4g sugars, 1g fiber), 11g pro.

READER RAVE

"Great taste! Would also work well with boneless chicken breast or thin-cut pork chops."
—GUNSLINGER, TASTEOFHOME.COM

STOVETOP TURKEY TETRAZZINI

A very special aunt shared this fun spin on creamy tetrazzini.
We think it's even better the next day.
—*Tasia Cox, Niceville, FL*

TAKES: 30 min. • **MAKES:** 6 servings

8 oz. uncooked spaghetti
2 Tbsp. butter
1 cup sliced fresh mushrooms
1 celery rib, chopped
½ cup chopped onion
1 pkg. (8 oz.) cream cheese, cubed
1 can (10½ oz.) condensed chicken broth, undiluted
2 cups chopped cooked turkey
1 jar (2 oz.) diced pimientos, drained
¼ tsp. salt
¼ cup grated Parmesan cheese

1. Cook spaghetti according to the package directions and drain. Meanwhile, in a large skillet, heat butter over medium-high heat. Add mushrooms, celery and onion; cook and stir until mushrooms are tender, 6-8 minutes.

2. Add cubed cream cheese and broth; cook, uncovered, over low heat for 4-6 minutes or until blended, stirring occasionally. Add turkey, diced pimientos, salt and spaghetti; heat through, tossing to coat. Serve with Parmesan cheese.

1 CUP: 420 cal., 21g fat (11g sat. fat), 102mg chol., 717mg sod., 33g carb. (4g sugars, 2g fiber), 25g pro.

CHICKEN WITH PEACH-CUCUMBER SALSA

To keep our kitchen cool, we grill chicken outdoors and serve
it with a minty peach salsa that can easily be made ahead.
—*Janie Colle, Hutchinson, KS*

TAKES: 25 min. • **MAKES:** 4 servings

1½ cups chopped peeled
fresh peaches
(about 2 medium)

¾ cup chopped cucumber

4 Tbsp. peach
preserves, divided

3 Tbsp. finely chopped
red onion

1 tsp. minced fresh mint

¾ tsp. salt, divided

4 boneless skinless chicken
breast halves (6 oz. each)

¼ tsp. pepper

1. For salsa, in a small bowl, combine the peaches,
cucumber, 2 Tbsp. preserves, onion, mint and ¼ tsp. salt.

2. Sprinkle chicken with pepper and remaining salt. On
a lightly greased grill rack, grill chicken, covered, over
medium heat 5 minutes. Turn; grill 7-9 minutes longer
or until a thermometer reads 165°, brushing the tops
occasionally with remaining preserves. Serve with salsa.

1 CHICKEN BREAST HALF WITH ½ CUP SALSA: 261 cal.,
4g fat (1g sat. fat), 94mg chol., 525mg sod., 20g carb. (17g
sugars, 1g fiber), 35g pro. *Diabetic exchanges:* 5 lean meat,
½ starch, ½ fruit.

⑤ CHICKEN PESTO WITH PASTA

Keep a container of pesto in the freezer. The next time you have leftover chicken, whip up this simple pasta for lunch or dinner.
—Taste of Home *Test Kitchen*

TAKES: 20 min. • **MAKES:** 8 servings

1   pkg. (16 oz.) cellentani or spiral pasta
2   cups cubed rotisserie chicken
2   medium tomatoes, chopped
1   container (7 oz.) prepared pesto
¼   cup pine nuts, toasted

In a Dutch oven, cook pasta according to package directions; drain and return to pan. Stir in chicken, tomatoes and pesto; heat through. Sprinkle dish with pine nuts.

NOTE: To toast nuts, bake in a shallow pan in a 350° oven for 5-10 minutes or cook in a skillet over low heat until lightly browned, stirring occasionally.

1¼ CUPS: 433 cal., 18g fat (5g sat. fat), 40mg chol., 239mg sod., 45g carb. (3g sugars, 3g fiber), 24g pro.

TEST KITCHEN TIP

Have an extra 10 minutes to spare? Make your own pesto! In a food processor, puree 1 cup tightly packed fresh basil leaves; 1 cup tightly packed fresh parsley leaves; 1-2 garlic cloves; ½ cup olive oil; ½ cup grated Parmesan cheese; and 1 tsp. salt. Refrigerate for several weeks or freeze in a tightly covered container. Makes ¾ cup.

**QUICK
CARBONARA, 190**

CHAPTER 7

PORK

Craving pork chops? What about tenderloin, bacon, sausage or ham? Watch everyone go hog wild for these tantalizing recipes.

❊ CHILI DOGS

People tell me I make the best hot dog chili around. It is timeless family-friendly fare that always disappears fast. These dogs are perfect for summertime cookouts alongside potato salad and your favorite chips.

—*Vicki Boyd, Mechanicsvlle, VA*

TAKES: 30 min. • **MAKES:** 8 servings (2 cups chili)

1 lb. ground beef
1 tsp. chili powder
½ tsp. garlic powder
½ tsp. paprika
¼ tsp. cayenne pepper
1 cup ketchup
8 hot dogs
8 hot dog buns, split
Shredded cheddar cheese and chopped onion, optional

1. For chili, in a large skillet, cook the beef over medium heat 5-7 minutes or until no longer pink, breaking into crumbles; drain. Transfer beef to a food processor; pulse until finely chopped.

2. Return to skillet; stir in seasonings and ketchup. Bring to a boil. Reduce heat; simmer, covered, 15-20 minutes to allow flavors to blend, stirring occasionally.

3. Meanwhile, cook hot dogs according to package directions. Serve in buns with chili. If desired, top with cheese and onion.

FREEZE: Freeze cooled chili in a freezer container. To use, partially thaw in refrigerator overnight. Heat through in a saucepan, stirring occasionally and adding a little water if necessary.

1 HOT DOG WITH ¼ CUP CHILI: 400 cal., 22g fat (9g sat. fat), 60mg chol., 1092mg sod., 31g carb. (11g sugars, 1g fiber), 19g pro.

☜ PIEROGI QUESADILLAS

One day I had nothing but leftovers in the kitchen, so I invented these five-ingredient quesadillas. Now it's how we always use up our potatoes and meats. You can toss in your favorite veggies, too.
—*Andrea Dibble, Solon, IA*

TAKES: 15 min. • **MAKES:** 4 servings

1 pkg. (24 oz.) refrigerated sour cream and chive mashed potatoes
Butter-flavored cooking spray
8 flour tortillas (8 in.)
1 cup chopped fully cooked ham
½ cup shredded cheddar cheese

1. Heat prepared mashed potatoes according to the package directions.

2. Spritz cooking spray over 1 side of each tortilla. Place half the tortillas on a griddle, greased side down. Spread with mashed potatoes; top with ham, cheese and remaining tortillas, greased side up. Cook over medium heat until golden brown and cheese is melted, 2-3 minutes on each side.

1 QUESADILLA: 630 cal., 22g fat (8g sat. fat), 49mg chol., 1559mg sod., 82g carb. (1g sugars, 6g fiber), 24g pro.

ASPARAGUS HAM DINNER

I've been making this light meal for my family for years, and it's always well received. With asparagus, tomato, pasta and chunks of ham, it's a tempting blend of tastes and textures.
—*Rhonda Zavodny, David City, NE*

TAKES: 25 min. • **MAKES:** 6 servings

- 2 cups uncooked corkscrew or spiral pasta
- ¾ lb. fresh asparagus, cut into 1-in. pieces
- 1 medium sweet yellow pepper, julienned
- 1 Tbsp. olive oil
- 6 medium tomatoes, diced
- 6 oz. boneless fully cooked ham, cubed
- ¼ cup minced fresh parsley
- ½ tsp. salt
- ½ tsp. dried oregano
- ½ tsp. dried basil
- ⅛ to ¼ tsp. cayenne pepper
- ¼ cup shredded Parmesan cheese

Cook pasta according to package directions. Meanwhile, in a large cast-iron or other heavy skillet, saute the asparagus and yellow pepper in oil until crisp-tender. Add tomatoes and ham; heat through. Drain pasta; add to vegetable mixture. Stir in parsley and seasonings. Sprinkle with cheese.

1⅓ CUPS: 204 cal., 5g fat (1g sat. fat), 17mg chol., 561mg sod., 29g carb. (5g sugars, 3g fiber), 12g pro. *Diabetic exchanges:* 1½ starch, 1 lean meat, 1 vegetable, ½ fat.

TEST KITCHEN TIP

To keep asparagus fresh longer, place the cut stems in a container of cold water—similar to flowers in a vase. Keep the asparagus in the refrigerator, changing the water at least once every 3 days.

HERBED LEMON PORK CHOPS

You'll receive plenty of compliments on these tender and juicy pork chops.
Mixed herbs and a final squeeze of lemon pack on the flavor in just 20 minutes!
—*Billi Jo Sylvester, New Smyrna Beach, FL*

TAKES: 20 min. • **MAKES:** 2 servings

1 tsp. salt-free garlic seasoning blend
½ tsp. dried basil
½ tsp. dried oregano
½ tsp. dried parsley flakes
¼ tsp. salt
¼ tsp. garlic powder
¼ tsp. dried rosemary, crushed
2 bone-in pork loin chops (6 oz. each)
1 tsp. olive oil
1 Tbsp. lemon juice

1. Mix seasonings and rub over both sides of pork loin chops. In a large nonstick skillet, heat olive oil over medium-high heat. Add the pork; cook until a thermometer reads 145°, 5-8 minutes per side.

2. Remove from heat; drizzle with lemon juice. Let stand, covered, 5 minutes before serving.

1 PORK CHOP: 200 cal., 10g fat (3g sat. fat), 74mg chol., 350mg sod., 1g carb. (0 sugars, 0 fiber), 26g pro. *Diabetic exchanges:* 4 lean meat, ½ fat.

TEST KITCHEN TIP

Here's an easy tip for keeping fresh lemon juice on hand. Squeeze the juice from several lemons, then freeze the juice in ice cube trays. When a recipe calls for lemon juice, simply defrost as many cubes as you need and use as directed.

5i ❄ HAM & SWISS STROMBOLI

A warm stromboli makes great game-day food or a welcome potluck contribution. It's easy to change up the recipe with your favorite meats or cheeses.
—*Tricia Bibb, Hartselle, AL*

TAKES: 30 min. • **MAKES:** 6 servings

1 tube (11 oz.) refrigerated crusty French loaf
6 oz. sliced deli ham
¼ cup finely chopped onion
8 bacon strips, cooked and crumbled
6 oz. sliced Swiss cheese
    Honey mustard, optional

1. Preheat oven to 375°. Unroll dough on a baking sheet. Place ham down center third of dough to within 1 in. of ends; top with onion, bacon and cheese. Fold long sides of dough over filling, pinching seam and ends to seal; tuck ends under. Cut several slits in top.

2. Bake until golden brown, 20-25 minutes. Cut into slices. If desired, serve with honey mustard.

FREEZE: Securely wrap and freeze cooled unsliced stromboli in heavy-duty foil. To use, reheat stromboli on an ungreased baking sheet in a preheated 375° oven until heated through and a thermometer inserted in center reads 165°.

1 SLICE: 272 cal., 11g fat (5g sat. fat), 40mg chol., 795mg sod., 26g carb. (3g sugars, 1g fiber), 18g pro.

APPLE-TOPPED HAM STEAK

Sweet apples combine nicely with tangy mustard in this dish to create a luscious topping for skillet-fried ham steak. I especially like to serve this in fall.
—*Eleanor Chore, Athena, OR*

TAKES: 30 min. • **MAKES:** 8 servings

4 fully cooked boneless ham steaks (8 oz. each)
1 cup chopped onion
3 cups apple juice
2 tsp. Dijon mustard
2 medium green apples, thinly sliced
2 medium red apples, thinly sliced
2 Tbsp. cornstarch
¼ cup cold water
1 Tbsp. minced fresh sage or 1 tsp. rubbed sage
¼ tsp. pepper

1. In a large skillet coated with cooking spray, brown ham steaks in batches over medium heat; remove and keep warm.

2. In same skillet, saute onion until tender. Stir in apple juice and mustard; bring to a boil. Add the apple slices. Reduce heat; cover and simmer for 4 minutes or until apples are tender.

3. Combine cornstarch and water until smooth; stir into apple juice mixture. Bring to a boil; cook and stir for 2 minutes. Stir in sage and pepper. Return steaks to skillet; heat through.

1 SERVING: 219 cal., 4g fat (1g sat. fat), 58mg chol., 1213mg sod., 25g carb. (18g sugars, 2g fiber), 21g pro.

READER RAVE

"I prepared this yummy dish the other night and we loved it. It is easy to prepare and tastes delicious. I used one large ham steak and cut it into serving-size portions for just the two of us."
—MARINEMOM_TEXAS, TASTEOFHOME.COM

PORK TENDERLOIN FAJITAS

These fajitas offer loads of taste appeal. Sizzling pork tenderloin and veggies are
coated with a zippy cilantro mixture and tucked into tortillas for a fun take on taco night.

—Rachel Hozey, Pensacola, FL

TAKES: 25 min. • **MAKES:** 4 servings

¼ cup minced fresh cilantro
½ tsp. garlic powder
½ tsp. chili powder
½ tsp. ground cumin
1 pork tenderloin (1 lb.), thinly sliced
1 Tbsp. canola oil
1 small onion, sliced and separated into rings
1 medium green pepper, julienned
4 flour tortillas (8 in.), warmed
Shredded cheddar cheese and sour cream, optional

1. In a small bowl, combine cilantro, garlic powder, chili powder and cumin; set aside. In a large skillet, saute pork in oil until no longer pink. Add onion and green pepper; cook until crisp-tender.

2. Sprinkle with seasoning mixture; toss to coat. Spoon onto warm tortillas; serve with cheese and sour cream if desired.

1 FAJITA: 327 cal., 11g fat (2g sat. fat), 63mg chol., 299mg sod., 29g carb. (2g sugars, 1g fiber), 28g pro. *Diabetic exchanges:* 3 lean meat, 1½ starch, 1 vegetable, ½ fat.

HAM & SCALLOPED POTATOES

I fix this saucy skillet dish often, especially when I'm running late, because it's easy and takes little time to prepare. The recipe won first prize in our local paper.
—*Emma Magielda, Amsterdam, NY*

TAKES: 30 min. • **MAKES:** 4 servings

4 medium potatoes, peeled and thinly sliced
2 Tbsp. butter
⅓ cup water
½ cup 2% milk
2 to 3 Tbsp. onion soup mix
3 Tbsp. minced fresh parsley
1 cup cubed Velveeta
1 cup cubed fully cooked ham

1. In a large skillet, cook potatoes in butter until potatoes are lightly browned. Add water; bring to a boil. Reduce heat; cover and simmer for 14-15 minutes or until potatoes are tender.

2. Meanwhile in a small bowl, combine the milk, soup mix and parsley; stir in cheese. Pour over potatoes. Add ham; cook and stir gently over medium heat until cheese is melted and sauce is bubbly.

1 SERVING: 353 cal., 17g fat (10g sat. fat), 56mg chol., 1170mg sod., 36g carb. (6g sugars, 2g fiber), 16g pro.

QUICK CARBONARA

Carbonara is a dinnertime classic, but my version cuts down on the time it takes to make. Loaded with ham, bacon, olives, garlic and Parmesan, it doesn't skimp on flavor.

—*Carole Martin, Tallahassee, FL*

TAKES: 30 min. • **MAKES:** 6 servings

12 oz. uncooked spaghetti
3 Tbsp. butter
3 Tbsp. canola oil
2 garlic cloves, minced
3 cups cubed fully cooked ham
8 bacon strips, cooked and crumbled
2 Tbsp. minced fresh parsley
¾ cup sliced ripe or pimiento-stuffed olives
½ cup grated Parmesan cheese

1. Cook spaghetti according to package directions; drain.

2. In a large skillet, heat butter and oil over medium heat; saute garlic for 1 minute. Stir in the ham and bacon; heat through. Add spaghetti and parsley; toss to combine.

3. Remove from heat. Stir in olives and cheese.

1 SERVING: 513 cal., 24g fat (8g sat. fat), 73mg chol., 1333mg sod., 45g carb. (2g sugars, 2g fiber), 28g pro.

TEST KITCHEN TIP

True Italian carbonara calls for pancetta, a salt-cured salami made from pork belly. Pancetta can sometimes be hard to find, so bacon is a good substitute. If you can find pancetta in your local supermarket, it's definitely worth trying.

TENDERLOIN WITH HERB SAUCE

Tender pork is treated to a rich and creamy sauce with a slight red-pepper kick. It's simple to prepare and always a dinnertime winner.
—*Monica Shipley, Tulare, CA*

TAKES: 25 min. • **MAKES:** 6 servings

2 pork tenderloins (1 lb. each)
½ tsp. salt
4 tsp. butter
⅔ cup half-and-half cream
2 Tbsp. minced fresh parsley
2 tsp. herbes de Provence
2 tsp. reduced-sodium soy sauce
1 tsp. beef bouillon granules
½ to ¾ tsp. crushed red pepper flakes

1. Cut each tenderloin into 12 slices; sprinkle with salt. In a large nonstick skillet, heat butter over medium heat; brown pork in batches, 3-4 minutes per side. Return all pork to pan.

2. Mix remaining ingredients; pour over pork. Cook, uncovered, over low heat until sauce is thickened and a thermometer inserted in pork reads 145°, 2-3 minutes, stirring occasionally. Let stand 5 minutes before serving.

NOTE: Look for herbes de Provence in the spice aisle.

4 OZ. COOKED PORK: 238 cal., 10g fat (5g sat. fat), 104mg chol., 495mg sod., 2g carb. (1g sugars, 0 fiber), 31g pro. *Diabetic exchanges:* 4 lean meat, 1 fat.

ZUCCHINI & SAUSAGE STOVETOP CASSEROLE

Gather zucchini from your garden or farmers market and start cooking. My family goes wild for this casserole. We like our zucchini grated, not sliced, but it's delicious either way!
—LeAnn Gray, Taylorsville, UT

TAKES: 30 min. • **MAKES:** 6 servings

1 **lb. bulk pork sausage**
1 **Tbsp. canola oil**
3 **medium zucchini, thinly sliced**
1 **medium onion, chopped**
1 **can (14½ oz.) stewed tomatoes, cut up**
1 **pkg. (8.8 oz.) ready-to-serve long grain rice**
1 **tsp. prepared mustard**
½ **tsp. garlic salt**
¼ **tsp. pepper**
1 **cup shredded sharp cheddar cheese**

1. In a large skillet, cook pork sausage over medium heat for 5-7 minutes or until no longer pink, breaking into crumbles. Drain and remove sausage from pan.

2. In same pan, heat oil over medium heat. Add zucchini and onion; cook and stir 5-7 minutes or until tender. Stir in the sausage, tomatoes, rice, mustard, garlic salt and pepper. Bring to a boil. Reduce heat; simmer, covered, 5 minutes to allow flavors to blend.

3. Remove from heat; sprinkle with cheese. Let stand, covered, 5 minutes or until cheese is melted.

1⅓ CUPS: 394 cal., 26g fat (9g sat. fat), 60mg chol., 803mg sod., 24g carb. (6g sugars, 2g fiber), 16g pro.

CARAMELIZED PORK SLICES

This treatment for pork tenderloin caught my eye when I was thumbing through a cookbook and saw the word *caramelized*. The flavor and ease of prep will earn this recipe a spot in your keeper files.
—*Elisa Lochridge, Beaverton, OR*

TAKES: 25 min. • **MAKES:** 4 servings

1   **pork tenderloin (1 lb.)**
2   **tsp. canola oil, divided**
2   **garlic cloves, minced**
2   **Tbsp. brown sugar**
1   **Tbsp. orange juice**
1   **Tbsp. molasses**
½   **tsp. salt**
¼   **tsp. pepper**

1. Cut tenderloin into 8 slices; pound each with a meat mallet to ½-in. thickness. In a nonstick skillet, heat 1 tsp. oil over medium-high heat; brown pork on both sides. Remove from pan.

2. In same skillet, heat remaining oil over medium-high heat; saute garlic 1 minute. Stir in remaining ingredients. Add pork slices, turning to coat; cook, uncovered, until a thermometer inserted in pork reads 145°, 3-4 minutes. Let stand 5 minutes before serving.

2 PORK SLICES: 198 cal., 6g fat (2g sat. fat), 64mg chol., 344mg sod., 12g carb. (11g sugars, 0 fiber), 23g pro.
Diabetic exchanges: 3 lean meat, ½ starch.

PORK VEGGIE STIR-FRY

A zippy sauce gently coats lean pork, peanuts and vegetables in this colorful stir-fry. Serve over hot rice for a simple and tasty supper.
—*Laurel Reisinger, Saskatoon, SK*

TAKES: 20 min. • **MAKES:** 6 servings

3 cups sliced cauliflower
3 Tbsp. vegetable oil, divided
2 medium carrots, julienned
1 can (15 oz.) whole baby corn, rinsed and drained
½ cup frozen peas, thawed
1 lb. boneless pork, cut into thin strips
2 green onions, thinly sliced
2 garlic cloves, minced
1 Tbsp. minced fresh gingerroot
½ to 1 tsp. chili powder
1 cup water
¼ cup soy sauce
4 tsp. honey
2 tsp. chicken bouillon granules
4 tsp. cornstarch
2 Tbsp. cold water
¼ cup salted peanuts
Hot cooked rice, optional

1. In a skillet or wok, stir-fry cauliflower in 2 Tbsp. oil for 3 minutes. Add carrots; stir-fry for 2 minutes. Add corn and peas; stir-fry until vegetables are crisp-tender. Remove; keep warm.

2. Stir-fry pork in remaining oil for 2 minutes. Add onions, garlic, ginger and chili powder; stir-fry until the pork is no longer pink. Remove; keep warm.

3. Combine 1 cup water, soy sauce, honey and bouillon in same pan. Combine cornstarch and cold water; gradually add to pan. Bring to a boil; cook and stir for 2 minutes or until thickened.

4. Return vegetables and pork mixture to pan; heat through. Stir in peanuts. If desired, serve with rice.

1 SERVING: 277 cal., 14g fat (3g sat. fat), 45mg chol., 1131mg sod., 16g carb. (8g sugars, 4g fiber), 22g pro.

ANGEL HAIR
PRIMAVERA, 210

CHAPTER 8

SEAFOOD & MEATLESS

If you're a seafood lover or just want to add a meatless meal to the dinner rotation, try one of these fresh and flavorful options.

CRAB-TOPPED FISH FILLETS

These fresh fish fillets are elegant and fuss-free, making them the perfect dish to serve company. Toasting the almonds gives them a little more crunch.

—*Mary Tuthill, Fort Myers Beach, FL*

TAKES: 30 min. • **MAKES:** 4 servings

4 sole or cod fillets or fish fillets of your choice (6 oz. each)

1 can (6 oz.) crabmeat, drained and flaked, or 1 cup imitation crabmeat, chopped

½ cup grated Parmesan cheese

½ cup mayonnaise

1 tsp. lemon juice

⅓ cup slivered almonds, toasted
Paprika, optional

1. Place fillets in a greased 13x9-in. baking dish. Bake, uncovered, at 350° for 18-22 minutes or until fish flakes easily with a fork. Meanwhile, in a large bowl, combine the crab, cheese, mayonnaise and lemon juice.

2. Drain cooking juices from baking dish; spoon the crab mixture over fillets. Broil 4-5 in. from the heat for 5 minutes or until topping is lightly browned. Sprinkle with almonds and, if desired, paprika.

1 FILLET: 429 cal., 31g fat (6g sat. fat), 128mg chol., 1063mg sod., 3g carb. (0 sugars, 1g fiber), 33g pro.

VEGGIE TACOS

Stuffed with a blend of sauteed cabbage, peppers and black beans, these tacos are so filling you won't miss the meat. Top with avocado, cheese or a dollop of sour cream.
—Taste of Home *Test Kitchen*

TAKES: 30 min. • **MAKES:** 4 servings

2 Tbsp. canola oil
3 cups shredded cabbage
1 medium sweet red pepper, julienned
1 medium onion, halved and sliced
2 tsp. sugar
1 can (15 oz.) black beans, rinsed and drained
1 cup salsa
1 can (4 oz.) chopped green chiles
1 tsp. minced garlic
1 tsp. chili powder
¼ tsp. ground cumin
8 taco shells, warmed
½ cup shredded cheddar cheese
1 medium ripe avocado, peeled and sliced

1. In a large skillet, heat oil over medium-high heat; saute the cabbage, pepper and onion until crisp-tender, about 5 minutes. Sprinkle with sugar.

2. Stir in the beans, salsa, chiles, garlic, chili powder and cumin; bring to a boil. Reduce heat; simmer, covered, until flavors are blended, about 5 minutes.

3. Serve in taco shells. Top with cheese and avocado.

2 TACOS: 430 cal., 22g fat (5g sat. fat), 14mg chol., 770mg sod., 47g carb. (8g sugars, 10g fiber), 12g pro.

LEMON-BATTER FISH

Here's a delicious classic. You'll love what the light and crispy batter does for your fresh catch. Just add hush puppies and rye bread, and you've got a complete meal.
—Jackie Hannahs, Cedar Springs, MI

TAKES: 25 min. • **MAKES:** 6 servings

1½ cups all-purpose flour, divided
1 tsp. baking powder
¾ tsp. salt
½ tsp. sugar
1 large egg, lightly beaten
⅔ cup water
⅔ cup lemon juice, divided
2 lbs. perch or walleye fillets, cut into serving-size pieces
Oil for frying
Lemon wedges, optional

1. Combine 1 cup flour, baking powder, salt and sugar. In another bowl, combine egg, water and ⅓ cup lemon juice; stir into dry ingredients until smooth.

2. Place remaining lemon juice and remaining flour in shallow bowls. Dip fillets in lemon juice, then flour, then coat with egg mixture.

3. In a large skillet, heat 1 in. oil over medium-high heat. Fry fillets until golden brown and fish flakes easily with a fork, 2-3 minutes each side. Drain on paper towels. If desired, serve with lemon wedges.

5 OZ. COOKED FISH: 384 calories, 17g fat (2g saturated fat), 167mg cholesterol, 481mg sodium, 22g carbohydrate (1g sugars, 1g fiber), 33g protein.

READER RAVE

"We've fixed this fish many times over the years and it always turns out perfect. The fresh lemon taste really comes through."

—2124ARIZONA, TASTEOFHOME.COM

GARDEN VEGETABLE GNOCCHI

When we go meatless, I toss gnocchi (my husband's favorite pasta) with veggies, Alfredo sauce and a dab of prepared pesto. I add zucchini sometimes, too.
—*Elisabeth Larsen, Pleasant Grove, UT*

TAKES: 30 min. • **MAKES:** 4 servings

2 medium yellow summer squash, sliced
1 medium sweet red pepper, chopped
8 oz. sliced fresh mushrooms
1 Tbsp. olive oil
¼ tsp. salt
¼ tsp. pepper
1 pkg. (16 oz.) potato gnocchi
½ cup Alfredo sauce
¼ cup prepared pesto
Chopped fresh basil, optional

1. Preheat oven to 450°. In a greased 15x10x1-in. baking pan, toss vegetables with oil, salt and pepper. Roast until tender, stirring once, 18-22 minutes.

2. Meanwhile, in a large saucepan, cook the gnocchi according to package directions. Drain and return to pan.

3. Stir in roasted vegetables, Alfredo sauce and pesto. If desired, sprinkle with basil.

1½ CUPS: 402 cal., 14g fat (4g sat. fat), 17mg chol., 955mg sod., 57g carb. (12g sugars, 5g fiber), 13g pro.

ANGEL HAIR PRIMAVERA

I love to make pasta primavera when summer is in full swing and garden-fresh veggies are at their best. You can toss in almost any vegetable that's in season. At my house, this dish is rarely the same twice.

—*Tre Balchowsky, Sausalito, CA*

TAKES: 30 min. • **MAKES:** 4 servings

1 Tbsp. olive oil

2 medium zucchini, coarsely chopped

1 cup fresh baby carrots, halved lengthwise

1 cup fresh or frozen corn

1 small red onion, cut into thin wedges

1 cup cherry tomatoes, halved

2 garlic cloves, minced

1 pkg. (4.8 oz.) Pasta Roni angel hair pasta with herbs

½ cup chopped walnuts, toasted

¼ cup shredded Parmesan cheese

Coarsely ground pepper

1. In a large skillet, heat oil over medium-high heat. Add the zucchini, carrots, corn and onion; cook and stir until carrots are tender, 10-12 minutes. Stir in tomatoes and garlic; cook 1 minute longer.

2. Meanwhile, prepare pasta mix according to package directions. Add to vegetable mixture; toss to combine. Sprinkle with walnuts, cheese and pepper.

NOTE: To toast nuts, bake in a shallow pan in a 350° oven for 5-10 minutes or cook in a skillet over low heat until lightly browned, stirring occasionally.

1½ CUPS: 416 cal., 23g fat (7g sat. fat), 22mg chol., 603mg sod., 45g carb. (12g sugars, 6g fiber), 13g pro.

TRIPLE CHEESE TWISTS

Our stovetop macaroni and cheese is extra special, thanks to the buttery crumb topping.
—Taste of Home *Test Kitchen*

TAKES: 25 min. • **MAKES:** 8 servings

1 pkg. (16 oz.) spiral pasta
1 small onion, chopped
1 garlic clove, minced
6 Tbsp. butter, divided
6 Tbsp. all-purpose flour
4 cups whole milk
1 can (14½ oz.) vegetable or chicken broth
1 cup shredded cheddar cheese
1 cup shredded Monterey Jack cheese
½ cup shredded Parmesan cheese
¼ cup bread crumbs
½ tsp. Italian seasoning

1. Cook pasta according to the package directions. Meanwhile, in a large saucepan, saute onion and garlic in 4 Tbsp. butter until tender. Stir in flour until blended. Gradually add milk and broth. Bring to a boil; cook and stir for 2 minutes or until thickened. Remove from the heat; stir in cheeses until melted.

2. Melt the remaining butter; stir in bread crumbs and Italian seasoning. Drain pasta; toss with cheese sauce. Sprinkle with seasoned bread crumbs.

1 CUP: 527 cal., 24g fat (15g sat. fat), 71mg chol., 644mg sod., 57g carb. (9g sugars, 2g fiber), 21g pro.

❄ CLASSIC CRAB CAKES

Our region is known for good seafood, and crab cakes are a traditional favorite.
I learned to make them from a chef in a restaurant where they were a best-seller.
The crabmeat's sweet and mild flavor is sparked by the blend of other ingredients.
—Debbie Terenzini, Lusby, MD

TAKES: 20 min. • **MAKES:** 8 servings

1 lb. fresh or canned crabmeat, drained, flaked and cartilage removed

2 to 2½ cups soft bread crumbs

1 large egg, beaten

¾ cup mayonnaise

⅓ cup each chopped celery, green pepper and onion

1 Tbsp. seafood seasoning

1 Tbsp. minced fresh parsley

2 tsp. lemon juice

1 tsp. Worcestershire sauce

1 tsp. prepared mustard

¼ tsp. pepper

⅛ tsp. hot pepper sauce

2 to 4 Tbsp. vegetable oil, optional

Lemon wedges, optional

In a large bowl, combine the crab, bread crumbs, egg, mayonnaise, vegetables and seasonings. Shape into 8 patties. Broil or cook the patties in a cast-iron or other ovenproof skillet in oil for 4 minutes on each side or until golden brown. If desired, serve with lemon.

FREEZE: Freeze cooled crab cakes in freezer containers, separating layers with waxed paper. To use, reheat crab cakes on a baking sheet in a preheated 325° oven until heated through.

1 SERVING: 282 cal., 22g fat (3g sat. fat), 85mg chol., 638mg sod., 7g carb. (1g sugars, 1g fiber), 14g pro.

QUINOA-STUFFED SQUASH BOATS

My colorful boats with quinoa, chickpeas and pumpkin seeds use delicata squash, a winter squash that's cream-colored with green stripes. In a pinch, acorn squash will do.
—*Lauren Knoelke, Des Moines, IA*

TAKES: 30 min. • **MAKES:** 8 servings

4 delicata squash (about 12 oz. each)
3 tsp. olive oil, divided
⅛ tsp. pepper
1 tsp. salt, divided
1½ cups vegetable broth
1 cup quinoa, rinsed
1 can (15 oz.) garbanzo beans or chickpeas, rinsed and drained
¼ cup dried cranberries
1 green onion, thinly sliced
1 tsp. minced fresh sage
½ tsp. grated lemon zest
1 tsp. lemon juice
½ cup crumbled goat cheese
¼ cup salted pumpkin seeds or pepitas, toasted

1. Preheat oven to 450°. Cut each squash lengthwise in half; remove and discard seeds. Lightly brush cut sides with 1 tsp. oil; sprinkle with pepper and ½ tsp. salt. Place on a baking sheet, cut side down. Bake until tender, 15-20 minutes.

2. Meanwhile, in a large saucepan, combine broth and quinoa; bring to a boil. Reduce heat; simmer, covered, until liquid is absorbed, 12-15 minutes.

3. Stir in garbanzo beans, cranberries, green onion, sage, lemon zest, lemon juice and the remaining oil and salt; spoon into squash. Sprinkle with cheese and pumpkin seeds.

1 STUFFED SQUASH HALF: 275 cal., 8g fat (2g sat. fat), 9mg chol., 591mg sod., 46g carb. (9g sugars, 10g fiber), 9g pro. *Diabetic exchanges:* 3 starch, 1 lean meat, ½ fat.

TEQUILA LIME SHRIMP ZOODLES

This tangy shrimp is a fabulous way to cut carbs without sacrificing flavor.
If you don't have a spiralizer, use thinly julienned zucchini for a similar effect.
—*Brigette Schroeder, Yorkville, IL*

TAKES: 30 min. • **MAKES:** 4 servings

3 Tbsp. butter, divided
1 shallot, minced
2 garlic cloves, minced
¼ cup tequila
1½ tsp. grated lime zest
2 Tbsp. lime juice
1 Tbsp. olive oil
1 lb. uncooked shrimp
   (31-40 per lb.), peeled
   and deveined
2 medium zucchini,
   spiralized (about 6 cups)
½ tsp. salt
¼ tsp. pepper
¼ cup minced fresh parsley
   Additional grated
   lime zest

1. In a large skillet, heat 2 Tbsp. butter over medium heat. Add minced shallot and garlic; cook 1-2 minutes. Remove from heat; stir in tequila, lime zest and lime juice. Cook over medium heat until liquid is almost evaporated, 2-3 minutes.

2. Add olive oil and remaining butter; stir in shrimp and zucchini. Sprinkle with salt and pepper. Cook and stir until the shrimp begin to turn pink and zucchini is crisp-tender, 4-5 minutes. Sprinkle with fresh parsley and additional lime zest.

1¼ CUPS: 246 cal., 14g fat (6g sat. fat), 161mg chol., 510mg sod., 7g carb. (3g sugars, 1g fiber), 20g pro. *Diabetic exchanges:* 3 lean meat, 3 fat, 1 vegetable.

TEST KITCHEN TIP

Our favorite way to make picture-perfect zucchini noodles is to use a spiralizer. At first glance, this contraption looks a little medieval, but it's easy to use. And the tool isn't just for zucchini. Spiralizers turn other firm vegetables, including sweet potatoes and carrots, into strands that resemble spaghetti.

🔟 LEMON SALMON WITH BASIL

At our house we opt for healthy foods, and this lemony salmon with basil is a knockout in the good-for-you category. We enjoy it with asparagus or zucchini.
—*Shanna Belz, Prineville, OR*

TAKES: 25 min. • **MAKES:** 4 servings

4   **salmon fillets (6 oz. each)**
2   **tsp. olive oil**
1   **Tbsp. grated lemon zest**
½   **tsp. salt**
¼   **tsp. pepper**
2   **Tbsp. thinly sliced fresh basil**
2   **medium lemons, thinly sliced**
   Additional fresh basil

1. Preheat oven to 375°. Place salmon fillets in greased 15x10x1-in. baking pan. Drizzle with olive oil; sprinkle with lemon zest, salt, pepper and 2 Tbsp. basil; top with lemon slices.

2. Bake 15-20 minutes or until fish just begins to flake easily with a fork. If desired, top with additional basil.

1 SALMON FILLET: 294 cal., 18g fat (3g sat. fat), 85mg chol., 381mg sod., 3g carb. (1g sugars, 1g fiber), 29g pro. *Diabetic exchanges:* 5 lean meat, ½ fat.

❄ CHEDDAR BEAN BURRITOS

My family goes meatless several nights a week, and this recipe is one of our favorites.
I usually puree a can or two of chipotles in adobo and freeze in ice cube trays so
I can use a small amount when I need it.
—Amy Bravo, Ames, IA

TAKES: 25 min. • **MAKES:** 6 servings

2 tsp. canola oil
1 Tbsp. minced chipotle pepper in adobo sauce
2 garlic cloves, minced
2 tsp. chili powder
1 tsp. ground cumin
⅛ tsp. salt
2 cans (15 oz. each) black beans, rinsed and drained
2 Tbsp. water
½ cup pico de gallo
6 flour tortillas (8 in.), warmed
1 cup shredded cheddar or Monterey Jack cheese
½ cup sour cream
Additional pico de gallo and sour cream, optional

1. In a large skillet, heat oil over medium heat; saute chipotle pepper, garlic and seasonings for 2 minutes. Stir in black beans and water; bring to a boil. Reduce heat; simmer, uncovered, until flavors are blended, 5-7 minutes, stirring occasionally.

2. Coarsely mash bean mixture; stir in pico de gallo. Spoon onto tortillas; top with cheese and sour cream and roll up. If desired, serve with additional pico de gallo and sour cream.

FREEZE: Cool filling before making burritos. Assemble burritos and individually wrap in paper towels and foil; freeze in an airtight container. To use, remove foil; place paper towel-wrapped burrito on a microwave-safe plate. Microwave on high until heated through, 4-6 minutes, turning once. Let stand 2 minutes.

1 BURRITO: 410 cal., 16g fat (7g sat. fat), 23mg chol., 726mg sod., 50g carb. (2g sugars, 8g fiber), 16g pro.

LEMONY SCALLOPS WITH ANGEL HAIR PASTA

This delicate pasta with scallops tastes so bright with a touch of lemon. Serve with crusty whole grain bread, and you've got an impressive dinner that comes together in a flash.
—*Thomas Faglon, Somerset, NJ*

TAKES: 25 min. • **MAKES:** 4 servings

8 oz. uncooked multigrain angel hair pasta

3 Tbsp. olive oil, divided

1 lb. sea scallops, patted dry

2 cups sliced radishes (about 1 bunch)

2 garlic cloves, sliced

½ tsp. crushed red pepper flakes

6 green onions, thinly sliced

½ tsp. kosher salt

1 Tbsp. grated lemon zest

¼ cup lemon juice

1. In a 6-qt. stockpot, cook pasta according to package directions; drain and return to pot.

2. Meanwhile, in a large skillet, heat 2 Tbsp. oil over medium-high heat; sear scallops in batches until opaque and edges are golden brown, about 2 minutes per side. Remove from skillet; keep warm.

3. In the same skillet, saute radishes, garlic and red pepper flakes in remaining oil until radishes are tender, 2-3 minutes. Stir in green onions and salt; cook 1 minute. Add to pasta; toss to combine. Sprinkle with lemon zest and juice. Top with scallops to serve.

1½ CUPS: 404 cal., 13g fat (2g sat. fat), 27mg chol., 737mg sod., 48g carb. (4g sugars, 6g fiber), 25g pro.

READER RAVE

"Made this last night. Didn't change a thing. Everyone loved it."

—MARK444, TASTEOFHOME.COM

CANNOLI
DIP, 252

CHAPTER 9

DESSERTS

Life is too short to pass up dessert, even on your busiest nights.
Surrender to temptation with one of these sweet treats.

CRISPY PRETZEL BARS

I often make a big batch of these peanut butter-flavored cereal bars on days that I don't want to heat up the kitchen. Kids especially love them, so they're great for picnics, potlucks and school bake sales.
—*Jane Thompson, Eureka, IL*

TAKES: 20 min. • **MAKES:** about 3 dozen

1 cup sugar
1 cup light corn syrup
½ cup peanut butter
5 cups Rice Krispies
2 cups pretzel sticks
1 cup plain M&M's

In a large microwave-safe bowl, combine the sugar and corn syrup. Microwave on high for 2 minutes or until sugar is dissolved. Stir in peanut butter until blended. Add the cereal, pretzels and M&M's; stir until coated. Press into a greased 15x10x1-in. pan. Cut into bars.

1 BAR: 74 cal., 2g fat (1g sat. fat), 0 chol., 50mg sod., 14g carb. (11g sugars, 0 fiber), 1g pro.

🟤 CREAMY PINEAPPLE PIE

Here's a light and refreshing dessert that's quick to make and impressive to serve. It's a luscious way to end a summer meal.
—*Sharon Bickett, Chester, SC*

TAKES: 10 min. • **MAKES:** 8 servings

1 can (14 oz.) sweetened condensed milk
1 can (8 oz.) crushed pineapple, undrained
¼ cup lemon juice
1 carton (8 oz.) frozen whipped topping, thawed
1 prepared graham cracker crust (9 in.)
 Chopped toasted macadamia nuts and additional crushed pineapple, optional

Combine milk, pineapple and lemon juice; fold in whipped topping. Pour into prepared crust. Refrigerate until serving. If desired, serve with toasted macadamia nuts and additional crushed pineapple.

NOTE: To toast nuts, bake in a shallow pan in a 350° oven for 5-10 minutes or cook in a skillet over low heat until lightly browned, stirring occasionally.

1 PIECE: 367 cal., 14g fat (9g sat. fat), 17mg chol., 185mg sod., 54g carb. (46g sugars, 1g fiber), 5g pro.

TEST KITCHEN TIP

Try this tip for a smooth, clean cut on a refrigerator pie. Warm the blade of a sharp knife in hot water, then dry and make a cut. Clean and rewarm knife before each cut. You'll have a picture-perfect slice of pie.

DEEP-FRIED COOKIES

My kids love this delicious, indulgent treat. I like to give the batter a
kick by adding a pinch of cinnamon and a teaspoon of vanilla extract.
—*Margarita Torres, Bayamon, Puerto Rico*

. . . .

TAKES: 25 min. • **MAKES:** 1½ dozen

18 **Oreo cookies**
   Oil for deep-fat frying
1 **cup biscuit/baking mix**
1 **large egg**
½ **cup 2% milk**
   Confectioners' sugar

1. On each of eighteen 4-in. wooden skewers, thread
1 cookie, inserting pointed end of skewer into filling.
Freeze until firm, about 1 hour.

2. In a deep cast-iron skillet or deep fryer, heat oil to
375°. Place biscuit mix in a shallow bowl. In another
bowl, combine egg and milk; whisk into biscuit mix just
until moistened.

3. Holding skewer, dip cookie into biscuit mixture to coat
both sides; shake off excess.

4. Fry cookies, a few at a time, until golden brown, about
1-2 minutes on each side. Drain on paper towels. Dust
with confectioners' sugar before serving.

1 COOKIE: 100 cal., 5g fat (1g sat. fat), 11mg chol., 123mg
sod., 13g carb. (5g sugars, 1g fiber), 1g pro.

🔵 CHEESECAKE BERRY PARFAITS

Nothing beats berry season in the summer. These fruity parfaits are an easy way to enjoy the flavor of cheesecake and a nice change from traditional pudding-based parfaits.
—*Patricia Schroedl, Jefferson, WI*

TAKES: 15 min. • **MAKES:** 2 servings

2 oz. cream cheese, softened
4 tsp. sugar
⅔ cup whipped topping
1½ cups mixed fresh berries
Additional whipped topping, optional

1. In a small bowl, beat cream cheese and sugar until smooth. Fold in whipped topping.

2. In each of 2 parfait glasses, layer a fourth of the cream cheese mixture and a fourth of the berries. Repeat layers. Top with additional whipped topping if desired. Chill the parfaits until serving.

1 PARFAIT: 146 cal., 4g fat (4g sat. fat), 0 chol., 1mg sod., 25g carb. (21g sugars, 3g fiber), 1g pro.

GRILLED BANANA BROWNIE SUNDAES

My niece Amanda Jean and I have a lot of fun in the kitchen creating different dishes. One of us will start with a recipe idea and it just grows from there—and so does the mess. That's exactly what happened with our Grilled Banana Brownie Sundae.
—*Carol Farnsworth, Greenwood, IN*

TAKES: 15 min. • **MAKES:** 8 servings

2   **medium bananas, unpeeled**
4   **oz. cream cheese, softened**
¼   **cup packed brown sugar**
3   **Tbsp. creamy peanut butter**
8   **prepared brownies (2-in. squares)**
4   **cups vanilla ice cream**
½   **cup hot fudge ice cream topping, warmed**
½   **cup chopped salted peanuts**

1. Cut unpeeled bananas crosswise in half, then lengthwise in half. Place quartered bananas on an oiled grill rack, cut side down. Grill, bananas, covered, over medium-high heat on each side until lightly browned, for 2-3 minutes. Cool slightly.

2. In a small bowl, beat cream cheese, brown sugar and peanut butter until smooth.

3. To serve, remove bananas from peel; place over brownies. Top with cream cheese mixture, ice cream, fudge topping and peanuts.

1 SERVING: 505 cal., 28g fat (11g sat. fat), 62mg chol., 277mg sod., 57g carb. (33g sugars, 3g fiber), 10g pro.

TEST KITCHEN TIP

Homemade brownies are divine. But if you want to speed things up, prepare a boxed brownie mix.

PRESSURE-COOKER CHERRY & SPICE RICE PUDDING

I live in Traverse City, which calls itself the cherry capital of the world. What better way to celebrate our wonderful orchards than by using plump, tart dried cherries in my favorite desserts? This pressure-cooked rice pudding is ready in a flash.
—Deb Perry, Traverse City, MI

TAKES: 20 min. • **MAKES:** 12 servings

4 cups cooked rice
1 can (12 oz.) evaporated milk
1 cup 2% milk
⅓ cup sugar
¼ cup water
¾ cup dried cherries
3 Tbsp. butter, softened
2 tsp. vanilla extract
½ tsp. ground cinnamon
¼ tsp. ground nutmeg

1. Generously grease a 6-qt. electric pressure cooker. Add rice, milks, sugar and water; stir to combine. Stir in remaining ingredients.

2. Lock lid; make sure vent is closed. Select manual setting; adjust pressure to high and set time for 3 minutes. When finished cooking, allow the pressure to naturally release for 5 minutes, then quick-release any remaining pressure according to the manufacturer's directions. Stir lightly. Serve warm or cold. Refrigerate leftovers.

1 SERVING: 202 cal., 6g fat (4g sat. fat), 19mg chol., 64mg sod., 33g carb. (16g sugars, 1g fiber), 4g pro.

NOTE: For a fun adult version of this dessert, soak the cherries in alcohol before using.

NO-BAKE PEANUT BUTTER TREATS

Perfect for road trips, this quick and tasty dessert won't stick to your hands. Keep them in the refrigerator for portable snacks.
—*Sonia Rohda, Waverly, NE*

TAKES: 10 min. • **MAKES:** 15 treats

⅓ cup chunky peanut butter
¼ cup honey
½ tsp. vanilla extract
⅓ cup nonfat dry milk powder
⅓ cup quick-cooking oats
2 Tbsp. graham cracker crumbs

In a small bowl, combine the peanut butter, honey and vanilla. Stir in the milk powder, oats and graham cracker crumbs. Shape into 1-in. balls. Cover and refrigerate until serving.

1 SERVING: 70 cal., 3g fat (1g sat. fat), 1mg chol., 46mg sod., 9g carb. (6g sugars, 1g fiber), 3g pro. *Diabetic exchanges:* ½ starch, ½ fat.

TEST KITCHEN TIP

Before putting peanut butter in a measuring cup, lightly coat the inside with water or oil. The peanut butter will slide right out without scraping.

WARM PINEAPPLE SUNDAES WITH RUM SAUCE

Pineapple, rum and sugar are already a flavorful dream together,
but adding ginger and butter really takes this dessert to another level.
—*Jamie Miller, Maple Grove, MN*

TAKES: 25 min. • **MAKES:** 2 servings

4 **fresh pineapple spears (about 8 oz.)**

½ **cup packed brown sugar**

2 **Tbsp. dark rum**

¾ **tsp. ground ginger**

4 **tsp. butter, cut into small pieces**

2 **scoops vanilla ice cream or low-fat frozen yogurt**

4 **gingersnap cookies, crushed**

1. Place pineapple in 1-qt. baking dish. In a small bowl, combine the brown sugar, rum and ginger; spoon over pineapple. Dot with butter.

2. Bake, uncovered, at 425° until the pineapple is lightly browned and sauce is bubbly, 8-10 minutes. Place ice cream in 2 dessert dishes; top with pineapple and sauce. Serve immediately with crushed cookies.

1 SERVING: 536 cal., 16g fat (10g sat. fat), 49mg chol., 221mg sod., 95g carb. (78g sugars, 2g fiber), 4g pro.

CRISPY NORWEGIAN BOWS

I've been fixing these cookies for so long, I don't recall where the recipe came from. They're a must at our house.

—*Janie Norwood, Albany, GA*

TAKES: 30 min. • **MAKES:** about 4 dozen

3 large egg yolks, room temperature
3 Tbsp. sugar
3 Tbsp. heavy whipping cream
½ tsp. ground cardamom
1 to 1¼ cups all-purpose flour
   Oil for deep-fat frying
   Confectioners' sugar

1. Beat egg yolks and granulated sugar until pale yellow. Add cream and cardamom; mix well. Gradually add flour until dough is firm enough to roll.

2. On a lightly floured surface, roll into a 15-in. square. Using a pastry wheel or knife, cut into 15x1½-in. strips; cut diagonally at 2½-in. intervals. In the center of each diamond, make a 1-in. slit; pull one end through slit.

3. In an electric skillet or deep-fat fryer, heat oil to 375°. Fry bows, a few at a time, until golden brown on both sides, 20-40 seconds. Drain on paper towels. Dust with confectioners' sugar.

1 COOKIE: 24 cal., 1g fat (0 sat. fat), 13mg chol., 1mg sod., 3g carb. (1g sugars, 0 fiber), 0 pro.

🟠 HEAVENLY FILLED STRAWBERRIES

These luscious stuffed berries are the perfect bite-size dessert.
You won't be able to stop at just one!

—Stephen Munro, Beaverbank, NS

TAKES: 20 min. • **MAKES:** 3 dozen

3 dozen large fresh strawberries
11 oz. cream cheese, softened
½ cup confectioners' sugar
¼ tsp. almond extract
Grated chocolate, optional

1. Remove stems from strawberries; cut a deep "X" in the tip of each berry. Gently spread berries open.

2. In a small bowl, beat the cream cheese, confectioners' sugar and extract until light and fluffy. Pipe or spoon about 2 tsp. into each berry; if desired, sprinkle with chocolate. Chill until serving.

1 SERVING: 41 cal., 3g fat (2g sat. fat), 10mg chol., 26mg sod., 3g carb. (2g sugars, 0 fiber), 1g pro.

CHOCOLATE MALT CRISPY BARS

This chunky, chewy square is a feast for your eyes.
Malted milk flavor coats each bar from top to bottom.
—Taste of Home *Test Kitchen*

TAKES: 25 min. • **MAKES:** 2 dozen

1   **pkg. (10 oz.) large marshmallows**
3   **Tbsp. butter**
5   **cups crisp rice cereal**
1   **cup malted milk powder, divided**
4   **cups malted milk balls, chopped, divided**
2   **cups (12 oz.) semisweet chocolate chips**

1. In a Dutch oven, combine marshmallows and butter. Cook and stir over medium-low heat until melted. Remove from the heat; stir in the cereal, ¾ cup malt powder and 2½ cups malted milk balls. Press into a greased 13x9-in. pan.

2. In a microwave-safe bowl, melt chocolate chips; stir until smooth. Stir in remaining malt powder. Spread over cereal bars. Sprinkle with remaining malted milk balls; press into chocolate. Let stand until set. Using a serrated knife, cut into squares.

1 BAR: 256 cal., 10g fat (6g sat. fat), 7mg chol., 118mg sod., 42g carb. (29g sugars, 1g fiber), 3g pro.

⑤ CHERRY-CHOCOLATE PUDGY PIE

Here's an ooey-gooey treat that's just right for campfires and cookouts.
You can also use blueberry or apple pie filling.
—*Josh Carter, Birmingham, AL*

TAKES: 10 min. • **MAKES:** 1 serving

2 slices white bread
3 Tbsp. cherry pie filling
1 Tbsp. chopped almonds
1 Tbsp. semisweet
   chocolate chips

1. Place one slice of bread in a greased sandwich iron. Spread with pie filling; top with almonds, chocolate chips and remaining bread slice. Close iron.

2. Cook over a hot campfire until golden brown and heated through, 3-6 minutes, turning occasionally.

1 SANDWICH: 309 cal., 9g fat (3g sat. fat), 0 chol., 294mg sod., 51g carb. (9g sugars, 3g fiber), 7g pro.

⑤ⁱ CANNOLI DIP

Ricotta is one of my family's favorite ingredients so it's only natural it makes an appearance in desserts. Scoop the cannoli filling into cones or break them up into pieces to use as chips and dip. The filling is also good served slightly warm.
—*Ann Marie Eberhart, Gig Harbor, WA*

TAKES: 10 min. • **MAKES:** 8 servings

1 carton (15 oz.) whole-milk ricotta cheese
¾ cup confectioners' sugar
1 Tbsp. finely chopped candied citron
1 Tbsp. grated lime zest
Mini ice cream sugar cones, optional
Miniature semisweet chocolate chips, optional

Beat together ricotta cheese, sugar, candied citron and lime zest. If desired, scoop ricotta mixture into cones and sprinkle with chocolate chips.

¼ CUP: 128 cal., 5g fat (3g sat. fat), 21mg chol., 70mg sod., 16g carb. (15g sugars, 0 fiber), 6g pro.

NOTE: Do not use a food processor to chop the citron—it could make it too fine, and its flavor is more intense with slightly larger bits.

RECIPE INDEX